Church as Network

Church as Network

Christian Life and Connection in Digital Culture

Jeffrey H. Mahan

An Alban Institute Book

ROWMAN & LITTLEFIELD
Lanham • Boulder • New York • London

Published by Rowman & Littlefield
An imprint of The Rowman & Littlefield Publishing Group, Inc.
4501 Forbes Boulevard, Suite 200, Lanham, Maryland 20706
www.rowman.com

86-90 Paul Street, London EC2A 4NE, United Kingdom

British Library Cataloguing in Publication Information Available

Library of Congress Cataloging-in-Publication Data
Names: Mahan, Jeffrey H., author.
Title: Church as network : Christian life and connection in digital culture / Jeffrey H Mahan.
Description: Lanham : Rowman & Littlefield, [2021] | Includes bibliographical references and index. | Summary: "The emergence of a digital culture has radically challenged assumptions about religious identity, how people connect and maintain relationships, and how people follow and give authority to leaders. This book explores the lessons digital culture offers as new types of congregational networks become popular and effective avenues for ministry"-- Provided by publisher.
Identifiers: LCCN 2021035480 (print) | LCCN 2021035481 (ebook) | ISBN 9781538135792 (cloth : alk. paper) | ISBN 9781538135808 (pbk : alk. paper) | ISBN 9781538135815 (electronic)
Subjects: LCSH: Church and mass media. | Social media--Religious aspects--Christianity. | Digital media--Religious aspects--Christianity. | Internet in church work.
Classification: LCC BV652.95 .M34 2021 (print) | LCC BV652.95 (ebook) | DDC 261.5/2--dc23
LC record available at https://lccn.loc.gov/2021035480
LC ebook record available at https://lccn.loc.gov/2021035481

♾️™ The paper used in this publication meets the minimum requirements of American National Standard for Information Sciences—Permanence of Paper for Printed Library Materials, ANSI/NISO Z39.48-1992.

Behold, I am doing a new thing; now it
springs forth, do you not perceive it?
Isaiah 43:19

For Sonora Elise Hyde, born into a changing world.

Contents

Acknowledgments

I am grateful to Iliff School of Theology for providing the opportunity to think deeply with students and colleagues about digital culture and the way it is changing how we think about religious practice. I appreciate my students' readiness to share their insights and experience, particularly those who read early versions of this work in class. I especially appreciate sabbatical leave where much of the heavy lifting for this volume happened.

Thanks to the Reverend Ian Cummins, who urged me to write this book, and to the generous lay and clergy folk who read and responded to various versions of this text. Among them are Meghan Johnston Aelabouni, Bob Bassett, John Hartshorn, Jerry Herships, Diane Hogue, Steve Kennedy, Otis Thompson, and Don Weinshenker. My nephew, Spencer Mahan, generously created the images used to visualize the shape of community in chapter 4.

I am grateful to the International Society for Media, Religion, and Culture, which brings together scholars from a variety of disciplines in conversations that have shaped my work. Several of these colleagues, and others with whom I work at Iliff, have read and commented on portions of the manuscript. Deep thanks to Heidi Campbell, William Dean, Jeremy Garber, David Hogue, Cathie Kelsey, Jeffrey Schein, Katherine Turpin, and Pete Ward.

I am grateful for Rowman & Littlefield's interest, particularly to Rolf Janke, who first saw the value of this project, and Natalie Mandziuk, who guided it to publication, for their support and engagement throughout the writing and production of this volume, and to the anonymous reviewers who responded to the proposal. They have been enthusiastic and encouraging partners. Some ideas and examples explored in this volume saw earlier publication in an article, "Congregation(s) in Digital Culture," which was published in the *Journal of Religion, Media, and Digital Culture.*[1] Thanks are also due to Routledge Press. Some of the ideas explored here were first developed in a religious studies–focused classroom textbook, *Media, Religion and Culture: An Introduction*,[2] and are further developed here for an audience concerned with the questions of Christian identity and community.

And always, Louise Mahan.

Author's Note

Church as Network is about the interactions of religion and media, particularly the way understandings of Christian identity, practice, and community are changing in a culture shaped by digital technologies, computers, and the World Wide Web. I wrote most of this book before the COVID-19 pandemic swept across the globe. Pre-pandemic, there was clear evidence that digital communication shaped the way we think about religious identity and community. Some people were developing new forms of Christian practice that responded to these changes. However, for most pastors and congregations, these things remained optional; they were not thinking about how media changed and/or shaped religious life and suspected that rich and meaningful religious life couldn't happen online. Thus, they used websites and social media to drive people toward their face-to-face gatherings. However, they didn't think much about whether Christian life could or should happen in online spaces.

Overnight, the virus changed congregations' relationship to media. Across America, congregations closed their buildings to practice "social distancing." Ill-prepared worship leaders rushed to learn new digital platforms and reflect on what an online service might look like. Chaplains and other pastoral caregivers began to imagine what their work looked like when it wasn't possible to visit people in the hospital, homes, and nursing facilities. Soon congregational meetings, fellowship groups, and study classes moved into digital spaces. Denominational office communications and pastors' Facebook groups and Twitter feeds articulated anxious concern for how Christian communities that could not meet face-to-face could gather for worship and service. Simultaneously, the pandemic highlighted the needs of the homeless, the undocumented, the persistently poor, and the newly jobless. It revealed fresh evidence of racial inequalities, not the least of which were those created or made worse by some people's lack of reliable access to digital communications.

What seemed for most a theoretical possibility, that our embodied lives of faith might find expression in digital space, has become a present reality. Perhaps by the time you read this, life will seem a little more normal. Hopefully, people are returning to work and worship in the material sanctuary, and we all have more regular face-to-face contact. But the post-pandemic world will be different from the world we knew before COVID-19. Part of what is new is a greater awareness that digital culture, with all its gifts and limits, continues to shape our lives. This awareness requires that we reexamine our understanding of the church and its missional commitments.

It is useful to know something about the author, their social location, and expertise in evaluating what you read. I am a straight white man, ordained in the United Methodist Church. From my childhood in a mostly white suburb outside Seattle, congregations have been part of my formation. I was a pastor of congregations in racially changing neighborhoods in Chicago earlier in my professional life. For many years, I have been a teacher of people preparing for ministry and community service. I continue to be rooted in a congregation's life and care about congregations and their future. My teaching and research focus on the images, stories, and rituals that interpret our place in the world and places where media, religion, and culture meet. I wrote this book to invite lay folk and clergy to think about how Christian practice is changing today, how changes in media culture contribute to changes in religious understanding and expression, and what effective ministry looks like in cultures shaped by the rise of digital media. I hope to support their vital work of imaging the forms of religious communities and communication that will be "good news to the poor" in digital culture.

Jeffrey H. Mahan
Iliff School of Theology

1

HOW DID WE GET HERE?

1

Christian Life in Media Culture

Like baseball, it seems quaint and less important than it once was . . .

This chapter introduces four key ideas that lay the groundwork for thinking about the challenges and possibilities that your congregation faces in a culture shaped by media change:

- Faith is a bodily practice rooted in a sensual encounter with the sacred. The divine presence is mediated by more than words. Protestants, shaped by print culture and focused on the Word and words, have a particular problem recognizing and adapting to other ways that the Spirit might be mediated.
- Christianity, like all forms of religion, is shaped by and responds to the media culture it emerged in and has adapted to media and other cultural change.
- People today live and practice their faith in a culture deeply shaped by the rise of digital communications, and this culture invites new forms of ministry.
- A digital metaphor encourages people to think about their identity, connection to others, and relationship to authority, and Christian practice as ongoing constructions.

The Christian life interacts with the media cultures in which it has been embedded. From its earliest days, the church has adapted to media change and challenged the assumption that media is simply a way of communicating unchanging Christian claims. Rather, just as Christianity takes different forms in different racial, language, and geographic cultures, so it has adapted to changes in media culture. Today, Christian communities are challenged by, and adapt to, the vast changes that digital culture is bringing about. To understand this, it is useful to put the rise of digital culture in the context of how faith communities have adapted to past media change.

The concept of *digital culture* refers to more than a new set of communication tools. The term describes the web of new possibilities and challenges that are created by computers and the internet. Online technologies lead us to reimagine how we date, take classes, shop, and gather information. Digital platforms offer new way of being and belonging. You may have online "face time" with loved ones or arguments with friends and strangers whether they are next door or across the globe. In digital culture, people are also developing new understandings of how God is active in the world, creating new practices of faith, and new ways of relating to other Christians and those of other faiths. This leads us to ask how our own understandings of the Christian life are changing and what the church will look like as its form and practices are reshaped by this media culture. Will congregations as we know them become irrelevant, or will they be reimagined in life-giving ways? Across the country, people are experimenting with forms of church that respond to the expectations that grow out of this new culture.

What do I mean by *digital*? Computers, particularly in conjunction with the internet, enable and encourage you to gather and integrate material from multiple sources and then make it easy to revise and reuse the things you have digitally constructed. To say that a literary text, an image, a piece of music, or other data is *digital* simply means that it is composed of bits. A "bit" is the smallest piece of information that can be processed by a computer and these are combined into "bytes"; similarly a "pixel" is the smallest bit of a digital image. These bits, bytes, and pixels are digitally rearranged by computers so that any digital text, image, or sound can be reformatted, combined with other digital information, and reused in other platforms. This is going on when a rapper "samples" and "mashes up" earlier pieces of music and uses them in new ways. It happens when you photoshop a picture, or when your pastor copies a section of her sermon and reworks it as a newsletter article or blog post. In a digital culture, nothing is ever final. Every text is searchable; it is available for review, and potential sampling and revision.

Because change and adaptation are inherent in "the digital," it becomes a powerful metaphor for the ongoing nature of creation. This metaphor influences the human imagination, including the religious imagination. As a metaphor, the digital invites us to reimagine the way we practice our faith so that it makes sense in, and speaks to, our context. In digital culture, it is not just texts, images, and music that are constantly being reworked. Steeped in a culture where everything is easily edited, transformed, and put to new purposes, we come to see ourselves as digital projects.

After Hours, Denver[1] is an example of the attempt to reimagine church in contemporary culture. They don't look like a conventional Christian congregation. *After Hours* does not meet Sunday mornings for worship; they don't organize programs for children and youth; and they are not interested in owning a building. Founding pastor Jerry Herships[2] focused them around two activities. During the week, a group of mostly (but not exclusively) young adults gather in a bar to talk about God, support each other, and make PBJs. The next day, some of them are in a city park serving the peanut butter and jelly sandwiches as part of a lunch for the homeless where they also serve communion. Out of this modeling of compassion and community, *After Hours* has built a network of folks who want to be involved. These groups include other churches as well as some seemingly secular groups: a law firm, a moms' group, a small business, a mergers and acquisitions company, and many more. Their level of commitment and involvement varies; some volunteer one time, others once a month, a few are there every week. *After Hours, Denver*'s network has grown to the point that someone, connected to *After Hours* in some way, is in the park offering a PBJ and communion every day of the week.

Whether in bars or the park, the community consists of those who show up. There are regulars and people who wander in. Further complicating the description of *After Hours, Denver* is their rich online life. A wider network of people, some part of other congregations and others not involved in the church, follow the pastor and *After Hours* online. They join in the conversation, pray for the ministry, and provide human and material resources to support *After Hours*' work with their "friends without homes."[3]

We can think of *After Hours, Denver* as a series of overlapping communities or groups of people that may never all occupy the same space. The folks meeting in bars on Monday nights make up one group. The friends without homes in the park are another. The followers online are a third group. Herships points out that there is a fourth group, the bartenders, servers, and other patrons of the bars where they meet. He says, "We never evangelize, but since being in these public spaces, I have been asked to baptize bartenders' kids, do pastoral care, and even marry some of them."[4] People move in and out of each circle, and sometimes between them. It is unclear how *After Hours* measures membership or participation to report back to its sponsoring denomination. However, that sort of counting would provide a very limited and misleading report of this experiment in Christian life's impact on lives.

Herships recalls that once he was out of town when someone asked through social media, "Hey Jerry, do you want a bunch of Girl Scout cookies for the Park? By the way, 'by a bunch' I mean a truckload." Jerry replies, "Sure, but I am out of town, we don't have any way to pick them up, or anywhere to store them." By the time Jerry returned to the conversation, people who participate online had arranged to pick up the cookies and found a place to store them.

These circles of occasional and regular participants soften the boundaries between who is, and isn't, part of a congregation. Their interactions illustrate the way social media complicates how we understand the idea of community and raise questions about what it means to "belong" to a congregation. People who study digital culture might describe *After Hours, Denver* as a network rather than as a location or fixed community. At *After Hours*, people are being fed, physically and spiritually. Is this a model of what church is becoming? I don't hold them up as *the* answer but as an illustration of how people come together to imagine the faith community in new ways. There are many other experiments in Christian communities going on across the country.

One way media change shapes relationships between clergy and their congregations can be seen in the casual and relational style that digital culture encourages. Online and in the pulpit, pastors share more personal information than they did in the past. The flow of information also means they know things about parishioners they would once have learned only in pastoral counseling or confession. Pastors must think about how these shifts in style and access to personal information impact the way they balance the personal and professional. What does it mean for a pastor to be a Facebook "friend" with parishioners? How will they protect people's privacy when they engage in these more public spaces?

REIMAGINING CHURCH IN CULTURAL CONTEXT

"Church" is a complex concept. We use it to signal several things. Sometimes we mean a particular congregation or the building where it meets, as when we speak of "the church I grew up in." At other times, we use the term to speak of particular denominations. At the same time, the term points to an ideal, to the connection that unites, or should unite, Christians of every time and place. As much as possible, I try to reserve the term for this last meaning and to say "congregation," or "building," or "denomination" when that is what I mean. To say that the church is an ideal is to say that it is something we imagine and toward which we strive. No formal or informal Christian gathering—as congregation, denominations, fellowship, study, or service group, as public demonstration, network, or flash mob—lives up to the ideal. Yet, at their best they strive to be church. What that means must be constantly reimagined as new contexts raise questions about how to live as though the realm of God were evident.

What do I mean by the claim that the church must be *imagined* and *reimagined*? Theologically, the terms are provocative and full of possibilities. They invite us to think about the church in the way the apostle Paul thought about the realm, or "kingdom," of God; it is both already at hand and also ahead of us as a possibility we cannot yet see clearly. In the evocative language of the King James Version of the Bible, Paul describes it as something we see "through a glass darkly" (I Corinthians 13:12).

The idea of church imagined and reimagined challenges the assumption that Christian tradition provides a single unified picture of Christian life. It suggests that Christian community exists as a series of contextual experiments. The *imagined church* is a work in process. It grows out of a vision of what the church might be while recognizing that we don't have it all figured out. The idea of the church *reimagining* reminds us that we are not the first to do this. Church as we have known it is a result of earlier generations imagining of what church might be in their contexts. In our times, when change is rapid and contexts shift, there seem to be more experiments with what Christian communities might look like.

Of course, our efforts to be church fall short of its possibilities, what we imagine does not live up to the fullness of the gospel. We are the inheritors of understandings of what constitutes church that no longer make contextual sense. Others are shallow. I once heard the host of an exercise program on an evangelical TV channel proclaim that her show was a ministry because "Jesus wants us to look nice in our outfits." While such an understanding of ministry is banal, other imaginings are evil. In Nazi Germany, some imagined that the church could serve the fascist state. Some Americans still imagine a church whose leadership is male and hierarchical. Attention to the complex relationship of religion and race in America reveals how the lens of white supremacy distorts the way many white Americans read the gospel and envision the church. We need to critique the limits and failures of these experiments and reimagine what the church might become.

Faith and Practice in Context

What do Christian identity and community look like for people shaped by a networked culture? How do they understand and express religious identity? How do they relate to one another and to their leaders? Do inherited church structures and practices shaped by an early communication culture serve or hinder their life of faith? Pondering the implications of cultural changes can help your congregation envision new models of church that more effectively engage the spiritually hungry.

Surely, some readers will counter, "we are the recipients of long traditions that guides our actions. To change the church is to abandon tradition." However, Christian tradition is itself fluid. We cannot reduce our rich and complex traditions to some rigid and universal orthodoxy of practices and beliefs. The broad Christian tradition is at times a chorus of voices blending and at other times more like a debating society. The tradition is women and men in different times and places who draw on, and challenge, each other as they work out what it means to follow Jesus in their unique situations. Engaging tradition need not mean embracing some hollow orthodoxy. Jaroslav Pelikan speaks to this when he says, "Tradition is the living faith of the dead; traditionalism is the dead faith of the living."[5] When we cling to tradition for tradition's sake, we lose the ability to bring it into conversation with our context.

This concept of a fluid tradition for a fluid church may seem entirely contemporary. Classic statements of faith, such as the Apostles Creed, seem today the summary of ancient consensus. However, they grew out of deep disagreements about how to understand the Creator, Jesus, the Holy Spirit, and God's activity in the world. The letters that make up most of the New Testament are addressed to communities facing unique challenges. Paul's letter to the Philippians (that is the followers of Jesus in Philippi) is intended to bring comfort to people who face suffering and persecution. In contrast, the letter to the followers of Jesus in Corinth (Corinthians) takes them to task for failing to live as a loving Christian community.

The legacy of who went before us is their effort to be faithful in their context. We in turn must be faithful in ways that make sense in our context. Christianity is better thought of as a quilt than a seamless blanket. Or, to draw on the image used above to describe *After Hours, Denver*, Christianity is a network of overlapping circles, distinct communities of Christian practice with both points of congruence and real difference. If we recognize that doctrine and practice have always been contested and contextual, we may feel greater freedom to imagine church in ways that reveal God at work in our day.

There are limits to what passes from one context to another. European and U.S. Christians once imagined they could export their cultural experience of Christianity to the Southern Hemisphere, and some continue this practice. Many Christians are now painfully aware that this form of mission substitutes the habits and mores of Western society for the content of the gospel. This masks the cultural and racial self-interest of the missionary and aligns the church with colonialism.[6] As African, Asian, and Latinx Christians strive to free themselves from colonial influence, they imagine culturally appropriate practices and emphasize different doctrines and beliefs than do European and American Christians.

For example, Western missionaries told converts among the Akan people in Cameroon and Ghana that the reverence for ancestors, which was part of their peoples' traditional practice, could not be reconciled with Christian faith. But today Akan Protestant theologian Kwame Bediako and Cameroonian Catholic theologian Jean-Marc Ela are bringing Christian concepts such as the communion of the saints into conversation with African traditional practices to imagine a distinctively African Christianity.[7] This sort of theological work seems to suggest that we in the West should be humble, respecting the ways Christians in other places reimagine church. Non-African Christians can learn from their work as we also imagine new ways to think about Christian tradition and bring it into conversations with our changing contexts.

From its earliest days, Christianity has been formed by, and responded to, the context of particular people. Our practice of faith is imagined and performed within particular social and political contexts with the media tools and metaphors available to us. Faith must adapt to the communications needs and norms of people in different contexts. The apostle Paul points to this in the way he adapted himself to the needs and forms of varied audiences. Paul "argued in the synagogue with the Jews and the devout persons, and also in the marketplace every day with those who happened to be there" (Acts 17:17, NRSV).

CHRISTIAN LIFE IN MEDIA CULTURES

In the discussion above, I claim that media change has so profound an effect that we can talk about *media cultures*. Further, I suggest that Christian life is shaped within particular media cultures, and particularly that we live in digital culture and must figure out how to be faithful and effective within it. Why should we pay attention to this? Because, if identity and community are shaped within media cultures, we cannot understand what it means to be a follower of Jesus today without considering our media context.

Here is one example of the influence of media change. More than fifty years ago, Marshall McLuhan, who wrote provocatively about the emergence of electronic media, discussed the decline of baseball as America's "national pastime." According to McLuhan the falling audience for baseball and the rise of football was a result of the effect of television.[8] McLuhan said that the rise of writing and reading made things linear, A comes before B. In contrast, in electronic media such as television, everything happens at once. McLuhan claimed that baseball reflected the culture of writing, one thing happened at a time, allowing the game to be described linearly. The ball is thrown, the ball is hit, the runner legs it to first. Football, he suggested, was an ideal game for television. The ball is snapped, and everyone on the field is simultaneously in motion. McLuhan predicted that media change made it inevitable that football would replace baseball in America's affections, and he has been proved right.

For McLuhan, more was at stake than our national sports preferences. He saw that the way television encouraged us to think was at the center of a cultural move away from the neat and orderly linearity of print culture to the messiness of a culture that requires us to pay attention to everything at once. McLuhan wanted us to see that in periods of media change, people develop new cultural practices that lead to new pleasures and encourage them to think of themselves and their relationships in new ways.

By now you may be thinking, "This is all very interesting, but what does it have to do with the church and its situation today?" Like baseball, a church that fails to understand the implications of media change loses its standing in the culture. It doesn't go away, but it seems quaint and less important than it once was.

We don't usually think about the role of media in shaping how we understand and experience our faith. But Christians are fundamentally storytellers: the way we tell stories about God, Jesus, and ourselves shapes our Christian communities. Therefore, before saying more about digital culture and its possibilities and implications, it will be useful to review Christianity's development through the lens of media change. Recognizing that media and Christianity have interacted over time in ways that still shape our practice of faith today prepares us to think about how our faith might respond to today's digital culture.

Oral and Written Religious Practice

Oral culture emerged as early humans developed the ability to speak and to understand one another. In the beginning, language probably articulated the basic human need for things like food, drink, shelter, clothing, warmth, sex, and sleep. More sophisticated uses of language helped them understand and express their emotional life and to negotiate about needs and desires. We see this same development on an individual level when a toddler begins to acquire words. First, simple phrases like "blankie" and "Mama" name key objects and people. Soon we urge the child to "use your words" to express feelings of affection, pleasure, frustration, or anger.

Oral cultures were changed by the gradual development of a culture of writing. This doesn't mean that the two did not coexist; obviously, we continue to speak and listen. The oral culture remained but was layered over and reshaped by a written culture that taught people and societies to think and practice in new ways. As we saw in McLuhan's discussion of the decline of baseball, writing encouraged linear thinking. For a long time, writing was a specialized skill. Documents were handwritten, with longer writings preserved on scrolls and later in handwritten and sometimes illustrated volumes much like the books we know today. They were expensive and rare.

The storyteller Jesus was born into a Judaism where most people were illiterate, yet their religious practice was shaped by their culture's embrace of writing and the technology of the scroll. Biblical scholars are divided about how likely it is that the carpenter was literate. There are only a few accounts of him reading or writing. In the account of "the woman taken in adultery," the author of John describes Jesus as writing in the dust (John 8:6) and, as was cited in the introduction, it is reported that he reads and interprets the Hebrew scriptures in the synagogue in Nazareth (Luke 4:16–21). Whether or not he could read and write, the Bible presents Jesus primarily as an oral teacher.

Very few of the common people Jesus traveled and taught among would have been literate. Followers of Jesus told stories about him and passed down his stories orally. Later, his followers adopted writing to preserve his teaching and the accounts of his public life. When he was no longer among them, letters instructing the emerging Christian communities were written, shared, and preserved. As the people who had known Jesus began to die out, varied accounts of his life and teaching were written down.

These early followers of Jesus embraced a new media technology that was superseding the scroll, the *codex*, in which pages were folded, wrapped in a cover, and bound on the spine, creating the book as we know it today. The cover within which the codex was bound protected delicate texts, and pages made it easier to access the contents. One no longer had to roll out the scroll to find the appropriate passage. Because it was easier to flip through the codex, it was also easier to read passages in the context of what came before and after it in the text. Eventually they gathered the diverse writings that had become sacred to their communities into the codex we know as the New Testament and bound it with Hebrew Scriptures to produce the Christian Bible as we imagine it today. At the time, most of his followers would not have been able to read them, yet together with Jews and Muslims, they came to be called "people of the book," that is, people whose relationship to God is articulated, preserved, and shared in a book that came to be seen as sacred.

Print and Literacy

The Reformation arose during one of the most significant shifts in media culture. The development of the printing press and moveable type in the mid-fifteenth century made reading material cheaper and thus more avail-able. This encouraged the spread of literacy, which is not surprising. Harder to predict was the way the new print culture would encourage people to see themselves as individuals and how this would impact the way people thought of religious identity and practiced Christianity. As McLuhan pointed out, learning to read taught linearity and causality, one thing comes before another. It has often been suggested that modernity rests on the development of these skills. It also had implications for how people constructed religious identity and understood their relationship to the Bible.

Before the printing press, books were hand copied by scribes, which made them rare and expensive. Hand-copied and illustrated Bibles were expen-sive. They were often chained to the pulpit, which visually underscored the clergy's monopoly on the interpretation of scripture. Then, in 1455 Johannes Gutenberg famously published the first printed Bibles.[9] Access to less-expen-sive Bibles would make the scriptures something that literate people could have in their homes and read on their own. This private Bible reading taught them to think of themselves as interpreters of the Bible and challenged the assumption that only the priest could understand and interpret the scriptures.

In 1517, only sixty-two years after the first Gutenberg Bible was published, Luther posted his ninety-five theses at the doors of the church at Wittenberg, an act that has come to symbolize the launch of the Protestant Reformation. It is an oversimplification to imagine that literacy alone caused the Reforma-tion; historians suggest that the plague, the rise of nationalism, the decline of Latin, and corruption in the church all contributed to the challenge to Catholic Christianity. But a central doctrine for the reformers was the primacy of the individual conscience, an understanding closely aligned with the sense of the reader as an interpreter. Thus, media change created the context for new understandings of religious identity and made possible the development of new devotional practices often centered in the home and family.

Today media changes as profound as those that produced the Reformation are reshaping the way we understand ourselves, engage the Bible, and relate to others. Hartford Seminary research[10] finds that congregations' adoption of digital and social media tools swelled in the first decade of the twenty-first century. At the turn of the century, about a third of congregations had web-sites while ten years later the figure was at 69 percent. Certainly, today the figure is significantly higher. The researchers reported that congregations that skewed younger, larger, or richer moved more quickly into the digital culture, but the research suggests that it's increasingly becoming an assumed norm. We should expect that increased experience with digital communication, both within their congregations and in their personal lives, will lead to changes in religious practice.

Material and Visual Christianity

It is easy, especially for Protestants whose tradition is so shaped by print and literacy, to forget that words spoken or written were not the only way in which Christianity was expressed. Christians also explore and express their faith through things they mark and make. Early Christian burial sites feature painted or engraved images such as crosses, doves, and laurel branches that recall biblical stories. Such images were inscribed on cups and graffitied on walls.[11] Later, great cathedrals were laid out in the form of a cross while their steeples stood as pointers toward heaven. Such church buildings are not just spaces within which people worship; they are physical expressions of faith. Today, in an art world largely severed from its ties to religious patrons, religious themes continue to find sensual expression through fine art such as composer John Rutter's sacred music, the Japanese printmaker Sadao Watanabe's well-known Last Supper woodcut, or the stained glass of Marc Chagall. We also see religious themes in popular art ranging from Norman Rockwell's *Freedom of Worship*, Christian-themed tattoos, to decals and T-shirts. Like the written word, this legacy of material and visual expressions is a part of our media inheritance. Our relationship with all these expressions of the divine is complex. They both express religious experiences people have had and teach them what sort of experiences of the Spirit they should expect.

The inside of the dome of Assumption of the Theotokos, a Greek Orthodox cathedral in Denver, provides an example that is suggestive of this rich visual and material tradition. A series of biblical figures painted on the plaster spiral down, illustrating the unfolding history portrayed in the Hebrew scriptures and New Testament. This sacred space is beautiful and instructive, but it is not conducive to preaching. Sounds echo and murmur under the dome. To Protestant ears, this sounds like a mistake. Yet, as incense rises toward the paintings and the chanted Orthodox liturgy reverberates under the dome, Christian faith is being expressed through image, smell, and sound in a quite different way than at the more word-centered Congregational church nearby. You can learn more about them at www.assumptioncathedral.org/#home.

Digital Media

Media that can be manipulated by computers revolutionize the way we capture and manipulate sound and image and make new ways of interaction possible. As with earlier media change, this brings new possibilities for how people will understand their identity, relationships, and communities. The rise of digital culture seems to be as significant as was the growth of literacy and the emergence of print culture in Gutenberg's day. A congregation for our era must imagine the Word at work in communities and cultures shaped by new media and be open to fresh expressions of Christian identity and community.

To align your congregation with digital culture, you must recognize that new digital communications technologies are not simply more powerful amplifiers for what was expressed in speech and writing. New media are reshaping our imaginations and practices. They alter the way we construct our identities and our relationships with others just as writing and later the printing press reshaped earlier oral cultures. Congregations must engage and be shaped by the new ways people in digital culture are thinking about themselves and their relationship to God. This will not be easy. Faith communities shaped by earlier cultural norms will not easily adapt or set aside assumptions that shape their practice of congregational life.

ABOUT THE SENSES

The Orthodox and Catholic traditions were established long before literacy was common. For them, the sacred comes through sensual experience. While each used and venerated hand-lettered Bibles, and their monasteries preserved libraries and scholastic traditions, for most people the experience of the faith was oral, tactile, and visual. It was known in the body. Worship involved ritual and procession. Smell, sound, and movement evoked devotion. Sacred texts were not simply containers for content; they were illustrated precious objects whose beauty itself evoked devotion. Clouds of incense opened the senses. Faith was expressed through icons, paintings, statues, relics, stained glass, and architecture. These things served as windows to the divine, and by gazing on them, touching them, or kissing them, people saw through them to the divine realities they referenced.

The Protestant Distrust of Image and Sensual Practice

The early Protestants, shaped as they were by writing and literacy, distrusted the material and were suspicion of the sensual expression of the sacred. We see this in the way that concepts like "word" and "book" shape Protestant thought and experience. The Radical Reformers rejected visual and tactile expression of faith, smashed stained glass, and pulled down statues in pursuit of a God who they believed was best experienced as divine Word and through words. In the process Protestants developed traditions that focus on having the right ideas about God at the expense of more bodily experiences of faith. This is not to say that Protestants haven't developed their own visual, material, and tactile practices. Yet Protestant suspicions of the tactile too often separate us from our bodily and material practices.

Every media change has unintended consequences. There are both losses and gains when a new media culture changes the way we think about the sacred, practice, and articulate our faith. One impact of the rise of literacy and the fascination with words and books that literacy spread was the sense that developed that the Christian faith was primarily a matter of belief codified in creeds. Thus, material and sensual experiences were downplayed, viewed at best as instructional forms that pointed toward the disembodied world of the spirit. Further, the material and sensual were often regarded as forms for the poor, for women, and for children.

The rise of writing and literacy likely encouraged an already long-standing distrust of the body and the senses in Christian thought. The body was long thought to be the location of sin, and the pursuit of sensual pleasure was understood to lead away from God. In contrast, the mind and spirit were seen as pathways to God. This binary split between flesh and spirit was reinforced early in digital culture in unfortunate ways. In the cyberpunk science fiction novel *Neuromancer*[12] the body is dismissed as "the meat." The novel imagined cyberspace as a place completely apart from the physical world where disembodied people could be whomever they wanted to be. Early computer programmers adopted this body-dismissive phrase, highlighting their sense that cyberspace was an entirely different and superior environment than the physical world. They and those who have studied digital culture have largely abandoned this distinction; they recognize that the self doesn't leave the body behind when going online and that people's online and offline lives are usually integrated.

This early way of viewing digital culture underscored unhelpful distinctions between the spirit and the body and the spirit and the material world that have not served Christian communities well. They have also often led to misunderstandings of actual religious practice. For example, much of the discourse about "religion online"[13] has imagined it as something completely apart from the embodied practices of people in congregations. Attention to actual people, congregations, and networks suggests much more integration of on- and offline religion.

MEDIA CHANGE IS PAINFUL

One of the challenges of adapting to media change is that people are imprinted with the norms of the media culture in which they grew up. Change is painful, and one reality of digital culture has been the speed of change. Recognizing the difficulty of change, we sometimes describe people who were formed by written and electronic cultures as immigrants to digital culture. They are portrayed comically in a Geico insurance commercial in which a woman makes a physical attempt to reproduce Facebook's digital "wall." She tapes photos randomly across her actual wall while her friend repeatedly exclaims, "That is not how it works!" The woman, and her fellow digital immigrants, intuit that some significant change is happening. They want to understand and participate but are anxious that the new media culture won't provide a substantial enough forum to maintain significant relationships.

It follows that people who have grown up in the emerging digital culture are "digital natives." They take as normative that almost everyone has a phone in their pocket that connects to the internet, that relationships are formed and maintained through social media, and they are sometimes baffled by those who cling to earlier ways of relating. The oldest of them are now in their early forties. They are not some strange outsiders the church should be in mission toward. They are already clergy and leaders in our congregations who long for a church that makes more cultural sense in the media world they inhabit.

What is true of individuals is also true of faith traditions and congregations. They are imprinted by the media culture within which they emerged. Those forms of expression seem to them the natural conveyer of the sacred. Institutions can be even less open to adaptation than individuals. Catholic and Orthodox expressions of faith were formed before the Gutenberg revolution. They continue to be shaped by oral and visual forms that are sometimes lost on Protestants whose traditions are so shaped by print and literacy. Media change does not have to mean that we abandon these media legacies. But those who draw on them must adapt to changes in media culture if they are to continue to flourish.

CONCLUSION: TOWARD A DIGITAL METAPHOR

In this chapter, I demonstrated that Christian faith has always been shaped by and expressed in cultural contexts and suggest that media are an important cultural factor that shapes how people understand themselves and practice their faith. This challenges the idea that Christians in digital culture are the first to engage the effect of media change. From its earliest days, Christianity has been shaped by media and media change. I have touched on the way orality and writing shaped Jesus's world and the way his followers embraced the *codex* (bound book) and later adapted to the influences of printing including particularly the rise of literacy. I suggested that the rise of literacy created a church of individual interpreters led by their understandings of the text and guided by their conscience. I also noted that this Protestant focus on having the right ideas likely lead to a distrust of more sensual experiences of the faith.

Like those who came before us, we live in cultures shaped by media change. We must understand this new communications technology and the culture that grows up around it, and figure out what a faithful practice of Christian faith looks like in digital culture. The way that texts, images, and music are constantly reworked, edited, transformed, and put to new purposes in digital culture encourages us to see ourselves as digital projects. This provides a fresh way to think about God's creative work in the world. Creation is not a one-time thing that happened in the storied past, but part of the Holy One's ongoing involvement with the created. In this process of Christian reimagination, we need not lose the rich legacies of our oral, print, material, and sensual inheritance. That is the stuff we will draw on, combine, and bring into conversation with the media culture of our day. Our religious identities and congregations are unfinished. God engages with us in the process of making and remaking ourselves and our communities.

DISCUSSION QUESTIONS

- In what ways does "religion seem quaint and less important than it once was" today? What remains compelling and relevant to you about your own practice of religion and the life of your congregation?
- How do the participants in *After Hours, Denver* look like a traditional congregation? What is different? How do they stay connected with each other?
- How is your congregation shaped by a culture of print and literacy? How does it embrace and resist digital culture? How might you *imagine* and *reimagine* the way your faith community practices and connects? Name one concrete idea for the future.
- How does your wider social context influence your faith community?
- What media does your community use? Name one possibility for new engagement with the senses that occurred to you in reading this chapter.

2

Church in American Media Culture

Both sender and receiver are modified by the message they receive . . .

I turn to the concept of *religious practice* to think about how people are religious or spiritual and to examine the way media has shaped Christian life in America. Here are the big ideas:

- A focus on religious practice, rather than on doctrine or belief, helps us see what Christianity looks like on the ground, particularly in times when media change evokes both adaptation and resistance.
- Noticing how practice has been shaped by media cultures challenges the idea that there is a fixed norm of the faith or a best media within which to express it. Understanding the multiple ways Christian faith has been practiced can reduce our anxiety about changes happening today and help us think about best practices for ourselves and our communities.
- The practice of Christianity in America has long been shaped by the way people adapted to media change.
- Understanding how the rise of digital culture encourages new forms of religious life helps us think about the possibilities and challenges for Christian communities today.

Describing the church from the perspective of *practice* puts the focus on what people do. In describing your own congregation, you would look for patterns of embodied faith that have endured or that change over time. This practice-oriented approach contrasts with one rooted in *doctrine*. Doctrine is prescriptive; it tells us what we should believe and what the church should be. Practice is descriptive; it acknowledges that what happens "on the ground" doesn't always match official doctrine or rules. Rather than seeing the shape of Christian life as already defined and unchanging, a practice approach assumes that in every time and place people and communities are working out what it is to be Christian.

Seen in this way, the church is a network of local experiments through which Christians seek to be faithful to the movement of the Holy Spirit in their context and to express the gospel as they understand it through the media available to them. Your congregation is one of those experiments. Tradition provides you with language, images, and experience that were useful in the past; it speaks of kings, shepherds, and virgins, invites you to fold your hands, to go on pilgrimages, to take care of the poor, and cast money changers out of temples. It is likely that much of this heritage continues to be at work in how you think about God's work in the world. Yet, in practice, some signs worked better for previous generations than they do today, and new language and practice emerges out of your experience. Tradition helps you attend to actions of the Spirit that you might otherwise miss, but it is not a rule book. What Christian life looks like, how Christian community is organized, and our vision of a just world are constantly being worked out and tested on the ground against the actual experience of communities.

Of course, practice can be idealized. Not all practice draws us closer to God. For example, attention to the actual practice of the congregations where most American Christians worship complexifies Paul's famous claim that in the church "there is no longer Jew or Greek, there is no longer slave or free, there is no longer male and female; for all of you are one in Christ Jesus" (Galatians 3:28). If we treat this as an accurate description of the church in Paul's day, and assume that it sets a standard for Christian life today, then most of us must acknowledge that we are not actually Christian or find ways to deny that sexism and racism live on in us and in the lives of our denominations and congregations. If instead we hear the passage as an articulation of hope for what the church will be, it invites a reflection on our practice that reveals the tensions between our striving to speak and hear a prophetic word in our setting and our tendency to treat our cultural assumptions about race, gender, and class as though they were sacred.

BELIEF AND/AS PRACTICE

It helps us understand the implications of *practice* to think about it in relationship to *belief*. Formal worship rituals like communion and baptism, the veneration of saints, foot washing, and going on pilgrimages are recognizable as religious practices. Practice also includes everyday spoken habits like repeating a table grace or saying "God bless you," and the gesture of athletes who point their finger toward heaven when they score. Faith-based works of charity and justice seeking are also matters of practice. Practice answers the question "Who are the Christians?" by considering what we do. In John's gospel, Jesus points to practice as the thing that defines Christians when he says, "By this all [people] will know that you are my disciples, if you have love for one another" (John 13:35 RSV).

Belief can be defined as a conviction or faith claim, such as a belief in God or the resurrection of Jesus. Creeds, such as the Apostles or Nicene creed, are attempts to summarize, publicly state, and teach matters of Christian belief. Belief, in this sense, answers the question "Who are the Christians?" by identifying the things we profess to hold in our hearts.

The relationship between practice and belief is complex. Sometimes it seems that people first come to believe and then develop a congruent practice. At other times, it seems that belief is an effort to describe what practice has already taught us. Certainly, examining our practice sometimes raises questions about whether we really believe the things we proclaim.

David Morgan, who studies religion, art, and media, roots belief in practice. He describes belief as "a shared imaginary, a communal set of practices that structure life in powerfully aesthetic terms. . . . a pervasive community of feeling . . . the felt expectation that the world works in a particular way."[1] Seen in this way, belief is not so much a matter of assent to particular creeds as it is the embrace of a shared world of practice and assumptions. Thus, to believe in the resurrection is to live as though Christ continues to be with us in ways that make a difference in the world. In what follows, I largely use phrases like "practice and belief" to focus on this "felt expectation" that underlies and is expressed in our practice. When you read "practice," I hope you will understand it to include this sense of belief.

CHURCH IN MEDIA CULTURE

There is no single right answer to the question of what the church should look like in digital culture. Congregations experiment with multiple forms of church, they bring resources from varied Christian traditions, and from their cultural context, into conversation with digital possibilities. Because understanding the culture around you helps you develop ministries that speak to people's needs, *Church as Network* invites you to think about whether and how your congregation is responding to media change.

People often speak of *the media* as though the term described something that emerged with modern electronic and digital technologies such as movies, telephone, television, websites, and social media. Were this so, the mediation of religion would be a modern phenomenon, and there might be some pre-mediated religious life that could somehow be recovered. However, humans have been using media in their religious practice from the time we began to use language and paint on the walls of caves. Werner Herzog's moving documentary film *Cave of Forgotten Dreams*[2] explores the thirty-two-thousand-year-old paintings in a cave in southern France through which ancient folk connected with the spirit world. It suggests that religion existed much earlier in human history than was once thought and that it has always been expressed through the medium of the day.

This connection between religion and media is most obvious when new forms of communication provide fresh locations for the religious imagination. Language, the capacity to make art, writing and the growth of literacy, and the emergence of radio, television, and the internet each did more than expand the range and speed of messages. Through these forms of expression people found new ways to relate to and articulate their experience of God and the realm of the spirit.

Certain practices seem to endure among Christians. We continue to baptize, to share communion, and in some way to worship and serve; yet ecumenical conversation makes clear that how we do these things, and what we think they mean, varies. The theological issues, forms of worship, and communal relations among the first-century Jesus movement, medieval European Catholics, Reformation Protestants, African Pentecostals, and postmodern American Christians are best understood when we give attention to their differences as well as their similarities. A theology of God as one who is continually creating and renewing helps us make sense of such fluidity and change.

What People Do with Media Technology

In thinking about the interaction of religion and media, it may at first seem that media are simply means of amplification, they send messages out to ever wider audiences. In this sense, writing made it possible to preserve and pass on a message to far distant people; printing made it possible to produce many identical copies of the message, making it available to many more people. Similarly, microphones let a speaker be heard by a wider circle of people, radio extended the circle, and tape recordings preserved the message. In this understanding of media, the religious messages and the ideas, practices, and experiences they communicate pass unchanged from one person to the next.

This amplifier analogy oversimplifies the complex process of communication. In actual practice messages do not travel unchanged from person to person. Rather, says philosopher Regis Debray, "both sender and receiver are modified from the inside by the message they exchange, and the message itself is modified by its circulation."[3] Further, messages do not travel unchanged from one medium to another. A written account of an oral exchange is not the same as the event itself, and image or sound recordings are different from each other and the written account. Media are not, in fact, interchangeable carriers of messages. Therefore, the media available to us shapes the way we are in and perceive the world.

The technologies of communication available to us matter. Yet, we misunderstand the process of communication if we only focus on technologies, as though a particular medium made some form of religious expression inevitable. We must also observe what people do with these technologies and how they and their messages are changed by the experience. Christian faith is formed and transformed in its communication, whether this communication involves a child hearing the stories of Jesus's birth, a pilgrim gazing at Michelangelo's painting of the creation of Adam on the ceiling of the Sistine Chapel, congregants mopping the brow of a Pentecostal "slain by the Spirit," or an interfaith Zoom meeting discussing the religious implications of Black Lives Matter. Paying attention to the way earlier Christians adapted to changing media cultures helps us understand their faith and its response to their cultural context.

In chapter 1 we saw that the movement that preserved the memory of Jesus made use of oral and written media. We went on to explore the way that the printing press, and the rise of literacy, encouraged people to think of themselves as interpreters of texts and by extension of themselves and the world around them as though they were also a kind of text to interpret. Transformed by their experience as readers and interpreters, people came to interpret the Bible and the practices of the Christian life in new ways, which transformed their understanding of themselves and led to new expressions of church.

Because literacy and print culture have lasted so long, it is easy to miss how they have shaped the way we Christians think and practice. This is especially so for Protestants; our tradition was forged in the rise of print culture. Print and literacy have so shaped our assumptions about the Christian life, that it is easy to miss the fact that earlier Christians understood their faith and practice differently. For them, oral and visual media provided a different religious imagination.

Because literacy and print had such lasting effect, it is tempting to think that they marked the end of media's effect on Christian practice. That is not the case. Subsequent media change also provided new opportunities for the religious imagination, and new media continue to reshape how we understand and practice Christianity today. The November 1861 edition of *Harper's Weekly* celebrated the establishment of a new medium, the transcontinental telegraph. The cover illustration is of an angel carrying a scroll and running along the telegraph wire. Jeremy Stolow suggests that "the electromagnetic telegraph invoked a coming age of free exchange and virtual telepresence. . . . By the time its cables had reached the Pacific Coast, the telegraph had already come to occupy a prime place in the American imaginary."[4] The telegraph was not merely a new and faster form of communication but a new metaphor for spirit at work in the world. The angel on the *Harper's* cover is evidence of a metaphysical hope that new ways of communicating create new possibilities for accessing the divine. Similarly, I argue that the digital metaphor outlined in chapter 1 is creating new ways of thinking about church and our relationships with other people of faith.

Resistance to, and Reflection on, Change

The magazine cover expresses an idealized hope for what a new medium might mean socially and spiritually. Nonetheless, people also resist media change. Some, after carefully considering the new culture that a new medium will encourage, decline to participate. Think for example of people who see the nastiness that social media can enable and opt out of reading and responding to Facebook, Twitter, or blogs. Others imagine only established media can adequately express the Holy; for them the sacred book is not adequately conveyed by a Bible app. Still, others lack the luxury of choosing whether to adopt or resist; they live where there is no high-speed internet or lack the money for smartphones and personal computers. It is also hard to imagine the possibilities of a new medium. It is said that when the telephone first became common, pastors had difficulty seeing it as a tool for ministry. They acknowledged that perhaps people would use it to make appointments for pastoral care, but they couldn't imagine that prayers or pastoral visits might be carried out on the phone.

It is wise to make an honest assessment of any new medium's potential contributions and costs. This is a complicated task since technologies have unintended consequences. Considering the response of the Amish to new technologies may be instructive. Those of us outside their faith community usually think of these traditionalist Anabaptists with their horse-drawn buggies and simple dress as resisters of change. It is more accurate to describe them as slow adopters. They are clear about their values and carefully evaluate the effects of new technologies, making principled decisions about whether and how to use them. When the telephone became available, they saw that it would be useful in business or in the event of medical or other emergencies. However, they also recognized its potential to disrupt family life and chose not to bring it into their homes. Instead, you often find a phone in the barn, business, or at the meeting place between several farms.

Today phones are pocket computers. They not only make and receive calls but also give us access to the internet and thus to GPS directions, games, and social media. When a family decides the age at which their children may have phones and whether anyone may bring them to the dinner table, they are assessing the potentials and possibilities of this form of media in light of their family values—just as the Amish did.

Congregations are also involved in this evaluation of the cell phone. My pastors long asked that we silence our cell phones to focus on worship and avoid interrupting the reflection of others. However, my congregation has now made it possible for people to give digitally, and phones often come out as we pass the offering plate. And, as the scriptures are read, some who like to follow along bring out their phones and click on a Bible app rather than turn to the Bible in the pew rack in front of them. When COVID-19 meant that we could not meet in the sanctuary, some people watched the entire service on their phones. So, my congregation—like many—is adapting to media change in ways that have altered our worship practices. The adoption of new technologies doesn't inevitably lead to superior forms of religious life. The use of our digital interconnection to give to the church and to access the scripture or even an entire service have the capacity to add to our worship experience, yet it is also the case that my neighbor's and my own phone are sometimes a distraction during worship.

American society is increasingly shaped by its relationship with telephones, computers, the internet, and other emerging media. This media culture is changing the shapes and patterns of our Christian life. Even when we are excited about the possibilities, we are often also anxious about what may be lost as new patterns of worship and relating emerge. Slow adopters remind us that media change has complex results. It's useful for religious communities to reflect on what sort of practices and relationships a new medium encourages and decide which are appropriate to their situation, values, and desires. Nonetheless, it is impossible to be entirely free of the implications of media change. As we consider the challenges and possibilities our churches face in digital culture, it is useful to remind ourselves of the way churches have dealt with cultural and media change in the past.

A SHORT HISTORY OF MEDIA CHANGE
AND AMERICAN CHRISTIANITY

The European colonizers imagined themselves to be extending the culture and religions of the countries they left behind onto the American continent. But they were also changed by their American experience. For British settlers in the seventeenth century, "home" was at best a twenty- to thirty-day ocean crossing, the voyage difficult and expensive; it took the Jamestown community four and a half months to cross the Atlantic. Emigration was, for them, a massive cultural and spatial change, and the American Revolution hastened the speed with which they and their children would come to think of themselves as distinctly American.

Theirs was not an ecumenical era. In the countries they left, Catholics and Protestants expelled each other as they came in turn to power. Anglicans ejected Puritans, and persecuted Quakers came to the American continent to establish a colony (Pennsylvania) where they would be free to practice their form of the Christian life. From its beginnings, Christianity in America took a diversity of forms and practices. Alongside these varied Christians were Jews and free thinkers and, though their religious traditions were largely unrecognized, the Indian nations. Enslaved Africans brought traditional African practices, and among them were the earliest Muslims on the continent. Later Asian immigrants would bring Buddhism, Hinduism, and other Asian religions to the Americas.

What unique forms of church would emerge as the colonists sought to express their religious identity and pass it on to their children far from the lands where they had been formed? The established communities from whence they came expressed their faith by establishing houses of worship and training and hiring clergy. However, the expanding frontier called for new temporary or occasional expressions of church. Colonists brought Bibles or other transportable symbols of their faith with them as they moved west. Many frontier families practiced family prayer and scripture reading. Larger gatherings of the Christian community were intermittent. Circuit-riding clergy visited communities and often led services outdoors or in someone's home. Baptisms and weddings would have been delayed until the pastor was available. People also traveled to camp meetings to hear revivalist preachers. These were experiments with what temporary form church might take on the frontier. It would require time and a growing economy for more established congregational life, and settled local clergy, to become the norm.

Religious life in America would also respond to new media technologies. Cheaper forms of printing were emerging, which led to the wider distribution of religious materials such as magazines, lithographs of Christian scenes, and hymnbooks. One practice, made possible by cheaper printing, was the production and distribution of religious tracts. Small, illustrated, and often printed on newsprint, they were inexpensive enough to be given away to strangers. Pointing to the way religion responds to both media and other culture changes, David Morgan writes that starting at the end of the eighteenth century, this "pious art" was distributed "focusing on children, immigrants, the poor, and laborers as well as prostitutes, drinkers, sailors, soldiers, infidels, gamblers, and theatergoers—all populations that Evangelicals felt were at risk in the emerging industrial revolution, which conducted a massive migration of peoples from the countryside to urban life."[5] Tracts could be handed out as part of face-to-face interactions or distributed anonymously by more introverted evangelists.

Never fully superseded by electronic and digital material, tracts are still available today and are typically purchased by Christians who leave them behind on restaurant tables, in public restrooms, or other places in hopes that non-Christians will find them and be converted. Readers may have come upon tracts that point to the end times and call for conversion. They are but one example of the unique religious practices being worked out in the interplay of religion, print media, and American culture.

Religious Radio and Television

The rise of radio and television, and the use of these media for public ministry, is illustrative of the possibilities and difficulties religious communities face in adapting to media change. As we have seen, media change leads to new understandings of the self and encourages new cultural practices. The rise of radio and television and the forms they took in the United States would enable new and uniquely American expressions of Christianity.

As with earlier media change, radio and television elicited both adopters and resisters among religious communities. Christian resisters were distrustful of these new media in two distinct ways: Social conservatives, who had earlier feared popular novels and the movies, saw narrative and music radio and television as "the devil's playground." Highbrow liberals dismissed them as "a vast wasteland." Each would have to adapt within a culture shaped by mass forms of electronic entertainment that brought stories, music, and sports into the home.

Evangelicals, with their high commitment to outreach, tend to be early adopters of new forms of media while the old "mainline churches," who were well established in society and well served by existing media, were more resistant. Evangelicals and fundamentalists, though distrustful of the popular culture that grew up around the movies, radio, and television, were quick to see the potential of these media as carriers of their messages, and their adoption of them has played a role in their growth in numbers and rise in social status in the twentieth century.

The first licensed commercial radio broadcasts were in 1920. Within a year or so Chicago preacher Paul Radner was on the air, and other preachers followed in their communities. There had been traveling revival preachers with national reputations before this, but radio made it possible for them to be in people's homes regularly. This encouraged the development of celebrity preachers with national followings. Preaching on the radio continues today, as you will hear on stations across the country.[6]

Commercial television adopted the genres that were popular on radio, offering comic and dramatic programs, news, and sports. Television spread quickly in the early and mid-1950s, and religious broadcasting quickly followed. Looking back on this history helps us understand the changes brought by the digital media of our day and the various ways churches respond to and resist these changes.

In the United States broadcasting was largely a commercial enterprise. However, the airwaves were regulated as a public resource and broadcasters were required to serve the public good. When the Federal Communications Commission (FCC) ruled that religious programming was one appropriate form of public service broadcasting, commercial stations began to donate studio time, and difficult-to-sell Sunday-morning airtime, to the dominant faith groups of the day, who were assumed to articulate widely shared religious values. The National Council of Churches (NCC), a federation of Protestant denominations, the Roman Catholic Church, and to a lesser extent Jewish groups produced public affairs programming with a religious focus, children's programs, and occasionally broadcasts of worship services for an audience assumed to share the producers' religious identity.

This system of religious broadcasting started to change in the 1960s. The FCC ruled that paid religious programming also met the obligation of stations to serve the needs of their communities. Then, during the Reagan administration, regulators stripped out most of the legal requirements for public service. In this era, religious broadcasting became a commercial enterprise.

Technologies continued to change; the rise of cable television, starting in the mid-1980s, radically increased the number of available channels. Where over-the-air broadcasting offered the three TV networks' national programs and perhaps a local station or two, cable had hundreds of channels, and cable developers were hungry for content. This made it increasingly possible for entrepreneurial religious groups to produce and market programming and even create their own stations and networks.

When free public access opportunities died away, the established religious groups largely withdrew from the world of Christian broadcasting. To be fair, there were efforts from the old mainline churches. In 1987, over twenty denominations and faith groups came together to develop the Vision Interfaith Network, later the Odyssey Channel, to provide religious programming to cable systems. Ultimately the experiment would fail, and by 2001 the production resources were absorbed into the Hallmark Channel, which offered minimal religious programming.

Perhaps mainline Christians felt so much a part of the general culture that they were not interested in a steady diet of religious programs. Confident of their place in society and suspicious of the entrepreneurial evangelical programming that was finding a market in the new television economy, the NCC churches, Catholics, and Jews largely surrendered the field. It is worth asking how that has contributed to both their reduction in overall numbers and the loss of the sense that they articulated a shared American set of spiritual values.

Previously dominant religious groups largely saw efforts to adapt to these cultural changes as an unfaithful acquiescence to popular culture and consciously and unconsciously resisted such changes. Evangelicals and Pentecostals were quicker to adapt to media change and seized on the broadcasting opportunities created by a free market. This contributed to their growth in numbers and as a social force in the United States. As their programs were exported, they also put an American stamp on the rise of evangelicalism in the developing world.

Where earlier mainstream broadcasters understood themselves to provide a service to fellow believers, evangelicals largely saw television as a way to reach people who need to be converted to Christianity. However, studies show that the vast majority of their audience self-identified as evangelical Christians looking for programming that reflected their religious worldview. This is not to suggest that evangelicals were not well served by their embrace of television. Programs like Pat Robertson's *The 700 Club* gave evangelicals, who had felt that they were a cultural minority, a clear home within the electronic media culture of the day. This moved them, in their own and ultimately in others' perceptions, from the margins to the center of society. In the public space of evangelical television, their language was spoken, their mores and values confirmed. Evangelical broadcasters increasingly addressed political issues and listeners, who had thought of themselves as a minority, came to see themselves as an organized "moral majority."

During the rise of evangelical television, many suggested that it would draw people away from congregations. While most of the audience maintained a relationship with a local congregation, the relationship was sometimes uneasy and competitive. Congregants came from watching the professionalism of Robert Schuller's Crystal Cathedral, Joel Osteen's Lakewood Church, or some other mediated megachurch, and wondered about the quality of the volunteer choir or the showmanship of the preacher in their neighborhood congregation. Local church advocates countered by pointing to the human connection they offer and argued that on television worship became a spectacle observed rather than a ritual of participation.

Typically, neither the religious adopters of television nor the resisters' response was rooted in a careful reflection on the cultural implications of media change. Anxious about media change and the new religious culture it enabled and burdened with class-based distrust of the television medium, the once-dominant old mainline denominations paid a significant price in cultural location for their failure to establish themselves in the new entrepreneurial media culture created by the deregulation of television.

Evangelicals were no more reflective than liberals about the cultural changes that entrepreneurial religious television would bring about. Evangelicals largely adopted the format of late-night television programs like *The Tonight Show* of the Johnny Carson era. Preacher hosts like Pat Robertson, Jimmy Swaggart, and Jim and Tammy Faye Bakker welcomed a series of actors, musicians, politicians, and sports figures whose celebrity legitimize evangelical practice and belief. In turn, the hosts themselves became celebrities and often adopted the excesses and entitlements of celebrity life as signs of divine blessing. The financial and sexual scandals of broadcasters like Swaggart and the Bakkers resulted in part from the unregulated celebrity culture that religious broadcasting encouraged and the inability of evangelicals to meaningfully regulate these powerful and increasingly wealthy independent religious entrepreneurs.

As we turn our focus toward the digital media of our day, what can we learn from this look back at the interactions of American churches with television? Americans now practice their faith in a culture shaped by television. The medium didn't replace face-to-face worship, but it did reshape it. Whatever decisions people make about which and how much media to consume, whether or not their congregation broadcasts their services or projects video in the sanctuary, their practices are shaped by the cultural impact of television. For good or ill, the ubiquity of television encouraged a society that operates under the assumption that people should be constantly stimulated and entertained. Television is said to encourage multitasking and shortened attention spans. In response, sermons got shorter, less expository, and more narrative in structure. Almost everywhere services are less formal. The pipe organ is being replaced by the accessible praise band. There is less tolerance of silent reflection and, perhaps, more attention to the visual, to image, and action, than was once the case in most Protestant churches. To be effective mediators of the gospel, congregations and clergy, whether consciously or not, adapted to the cultural changes that television encourages. Today they need to respond to a culture shaped by digital communications and the internet.

IMPLICATIONS OF DIGITAL MEDIA FOR RELIGIOUS PRACTICE

We tend to think of new forms of media through the lens of the medium that proceeded them. Recorded music first simply captured live performance. As people lived into the possibilities of the recording studio, music was created that couldn't be duplicated onstage. Similarly, when the internet first emerged, people saw it as a giant library that gave us access to unimaginably more texts than ever before. We thought of it through the logic of a written culture in which a few people with authority were writers and the rest of us were readers. With the rise of what is often called Internet 2.0, people begun to imagine it differently. Rather than thinking of the internet as a library of texts, they see it as a discussion and performance space. Within this internet space, receivers respond to, challenge, revise, and repurpose messages. New identities and relationships were explored. Today, interaction is the point when you blog, tweet, or post something on Facebook. If no one responds you have failed.

Interactivity encourages a different understanding of what it means to be an authority. People acculturated to the interactive conversational style of internet communication are unlikely to respond well to top-down communication. Too often religious and other leaders try to use the internet and social media as though they are merely better amplifiers of one-way communication. However, congregations and their leaders who understand this new media culture see the internet as a place where they will have different kinds of relationships with people.

Wikipedia illustrates the implications of new digital media. A wiki is a living repository of information. Someone posts an entry, perhaps creating a page describing a religious movement or discussing a theological topic. Every reader of that post is a potential editor, free to correct, expand, or change the entry. This process is unending; the entry is public but never finished. Old understandings of author and audience are challenged and soon we cannot easily answer the question, "who is the author of the entry?"

What are the implications of this media culture for congregations? The vast library was and is useful to the life of the church. You can, for instance, respond to the earlier discussion of the Gutenberg Bible by going online and finding images of pages from that historic document. You can also find images of the Dead Sea scrolls and medieval illustrated Bibles to illustrate the forms the Bible took before Gutenberg. Used in this way, the internet speeds up our access and makes a wider range of material accessible. Most churches continue to use the new media as an extension of the old media that has shaped their self-understanding and practice. Leaders treat it as a one-way form of communication that amplifies their messages. However, congregations and their leaders who embrace the internet as a space for conversation, play, and experiment, see that it makes possible new forms of community and invites more conversational relationships. The conversational communities of the internet, and wiki in which we are all potential authors and editors, provide a further clarifying metaphor for how people will think of church as they adapt to digital culture.

Christian Life in the Digital Age

The digitization of image and information, the emergence and development of the internet, and the rise of various forms of social media are elements of the most recent media revolution. As with past media change, questions arise. What does religion look like during this monumental shift? How do individuals, movements, and institutions adapt to the new communication technologies that rapidly divide text and image into infinitely variable building blocks, create new "spaces" and relationships, and allow data to be sampled, edited, and reorganized with the click of a mouse? What sort of persons and societies are we becoming, and what forms of Christian practice are emerging that speak of the ineffable sacred in these new media spaces? And what are the implications of this for your congregation? The digital as a metaphor helps us make sense of religious practice in this media culture. When the very notion of "digital" implies that images, practices, and texts can be broken down into small pieces, it follows that the pieces can be extracted and reused in ways that reimagine the logic of the original system. Religious lives and congregations are ongoing constructions being made and remade in response to our spiritual, economic, and political contexts.

When people, informed by their experience of blogging, social media, and wiki construction, think about the church and their Christian faith, they are unlikely to think of themselves as simply the recipients of some authority's insights about Christian texts and practices, or as tied to a single institution or practice. They have complex networked relationships and are less likely to be joiners of sororities, bowling leagues, fraternal organizations like the Masons, or congregations. The new media culture encourages more complex, if sometimes more ephemeral, relationships. People want to connect and have substantive experiences together, but these old centers of life are likely to be but one of many overlapping circles of relationship.

As media technologies change and new forms become cheaper and simpler to use, they become available to a wider range of people. When people outside the traditional centers of religious authority begin to master new forms of communication, the web provides space for experimentation and as in the Reformation before us, new forms of Christian practice and belief are developed and tested. Old models of authority will be affected as new voices emerge.

The point is not that your congregation must adopt every new form of media in their personal and religious lives, that only Luddites resist media change. Rather, individuals and congregations need to understand how American society is adapting in response to new media. Decisions about which forms of media to use are always contextual and aesthetic decisions. Yet, in the media culture we inhabit, it is necessary to pay attention to the way people, communities, and institutions mediate their faith to recognize evolving forms of Christian life today.

The chapters that follow identify and explore cultural shifts related to media change. If people are changing the way they construct their religious lives, how they connect with others in networked communities, and how they relate to sages and leaders, the church will have to adapt to connect with them in meaningful ways. Your congregation will be more effective if you are intentional about how you are interacting with our emerging digital context.

Put this book in dialogue with the understandings of church that grow out of your theology and cultural context to help you imagine what effective Christian community and practice look like in your setting. The church that is emerging in digital culture exists as a range of possibilities. It is in the process of becoming, and it will take multiple forms. The Spirit will be at work among God's people in emerging digital cultures, and it behooves us to recognize that we will need to struggle with the desire to idealize these new forms of church as well as with hollow orthodoxies and prejudices if we are to find liberating ways to gather for Christian worship, community, and service in our new cultural context.

DISCUSSION QUESTIONS

- How does "practice" differ from "faith" or "belief"? Does this distinction help to describe your own religious life and/or the shared life of your congregation? If so, how?
- How was the Christian faith communicated to you in words, images, and practices?
- Name a major influence of media from the story of your faith tradition or community.
- How does your community use digital media? Which forms of digital media have you considered and, like the Amish, either not used or used in limited ways? Why?

II

RELIGION AND SPIRITUALITY IN DIGITAL CULTURE

3

Constructing Religious Identity

Should a Christian fly Buddhist prayer flags?

This chapter suggests that today's religious lives seem focused on the construction and performance of personal religious identity, a practice modeled and encouraged by digital culture. Here are four main ideas we will explore:

- Religious identity once seemed largely unchanging, a role or way of being received from family and community. Today, religious identity seems fluid and less settled, a lifelong individual project.
- The digital metaphor introduced earlier suggests that the ease with which digital technologies allow us to access and edit texts provides a way to think about the fluid religious self. Here concepts of hyphenation, sampling, and mashup extend the discussion of what this looks like in practice.
- This focus on identity construction looks more to the future than to the past. From this perspective, tradition is a library or supermarket from which people can select and combine elements that together express their religious identity.
- Finally, gathering and organizing the elements that make up a religious identity involves processes of spiritual consumption through which people gather material, images, and practices and rework them to construct an individual religious identity.

If your congregation sees itself as the steward of a faith tradition, it may confound you to discover that people feel free to choose which spiritual practices and beliefs they will adopt. This freedom challenges the community's role and authority. This can leave you with questions about how to help these religious free spirits.

A former student tells a story that illustrates the change. Meeting with a couple who want their child baptized, he shares the statement of faith the denomination's baptismal liturgy asks parents to make. The young father points to a line that expresses a relatively high theological claim about Jesus's divinity, and announces, "I can't say *that*." So, the pastor helps the couple clarify what they believe and rewrites the liturgy to express what they can say with integrity about Jesus and what it means for them to follow him.

Baptism serves as an opportunity for the couple to clarify their faith and practice and to relate to a caring pastor and congregation. Both the pastor and I are pleased to have someone take the liturgy that seriously. Yet, as we seek to understand what religious identity looks like today, we ought to notice what is happening in that negotiation. The pastor and parents treat Christian identity as a personal construction. They do not see it as a seamless whole or system that ties the practitioner to a particular community. Instead, they view the faith tradition as collections of resources that individuals can adapt to serve personal spiritual projects.

I don't repeat this story to attack their negotiation of Christian claims and practices but to recognize that it is a norm of contemporary religious life. Their thoughtful theological discussion reminds me of a story told about Mark Twain. He was supposedly asked, "Do you believe in infant baptism?" Twain replied, "Believe in it? Hell, I have seen it done." Twain's humorous reply reminded us that regardless of whether we approve of the practice, it is one way people are living out Christian lives. Let his response to the question about infant baptism sit in the background, a witty—if not entirely adequate—reminder, as you think about how people create and articulate religious identity today.

CONSTRUCTING IDENTITIES

Digital technology allows you to sample, edit, and alter words, images, or music from various sources and combining them in new ways that lead to fresh insights. Not long ago, this required highly technical skill; it was something done by media professionals. Today, schoolchildren do it. A new movie or TV show comes out, and immediately GIFs created from crucial moments are redeployed as online discussion comments. A middle school youth group's adult leader posts a last-minute warning that their outing might get rain. A sixth grader responds with an image from the Netflix series, *Umbrella Academy*, in which an actor opens and twirls a red umbrella. This creative reuse of media is an everyday occurrence.

The way digital technologies allow you to edit and creatively reuse material shapes the way people think about their religious identity. People see their own lives as analogous to digital images, sounds, and texts. Thus, identity is constructed from gathered material and experiences and subject to ongoing reconstruction. Pastoral theologian David Hogue suggests that narrative theologies (and psychologies) share this assumption. Therapists encourage us to "rewrite" our personal stories.[1] Each of us is an editor who seeks to produce a next edition of the self that is clearer and more beautiful.

This can be messy. A faculty colleague responds to the display of a string of tiny colorful prayer flags by someone who identifies as Christian by asking, "Should a Christian fly Buddhist prayer flags?" After all, Christianity and Buddhism have different assumptions about crucial matters, such as what happens when we die and whether there is a deity. He wonders how the individual resolves these differences.

I appreciate his desire for religious identity and practice to cohere to a theological center. Yet, as one scholar has observed in reflecting on religion in digital culture, religious authorities "no longer control their own signs and symbols."[2] It is not uncommon for people today to incorporate elements from other tradition into their Christian practice. Though it may make both Buddhists and Christians uncomfortable, prayer flags and Buddhist meditation are part of the spiritual lives of some people who understand themselves to be Christian, and others who understand themselves to be simultaneously Buddhist and Christian. Constructive theological work is needed to better understand these performances of belief and practice.[3]

You may have mixed reactions to hearing that some Christians adopt Buddhist practices or that some Protestants adopt Catholic prayer practice. How shall we understand this? Whether you accept this as an uncontroversial result of interreligious exposure and conversation or worry that it obscures traditional Christian (and Buddhist) practice, like Twain's infant baptism you have "seen it done."

TRADITION IN A TIME OF RECONSTRUCTION

No one constructs identity in a void. In creating the religious self, you model yourself on religious figures you emulate and seek to unlearn patterns, vocabularies, and sensations you find oppressive. These things have histories. Even if you give little authority to tradition, it provides the source material you sample and reuse to construct and perform your religious identity.

Thinking about tradition helps us make sense of religious identity making. The concept of a religious tradition suggests a shared story embedded in common bodily actions, images, language, and ideas. By participating in a faith tradition, you inherit the distinctive practices and interpretations that sets your community apart from others. For instance, though both Roman Catholics and Mennonites offer communion, they have different theological understandings of the ritual. For Mennonites, "the Lord's Supper is a *sign* by which the church thankfully remembers the new covenant which Jesus established by his death."[4] This distinguishes them from Catholics, who believe that the bread and wine are changed to be the actual body and blood of Jesus (transubstantiation).

Religious traditions are shaped by what is happening in society. For example, Black people's African heritage and the experiences of slavery and racism produced specific theologies and forms of worship and prayer rooted in their experience. Though they are less likely to recognize it, it is equally the case that white Christians' quite different experience of race shapes their religion, sometimes excluding people of color and treating white privilege as though it were a doctrine of faith.

We express fidelity to a particular community both by embracing its distinctive practices and avoiding others. For my rural Methodist grandparents, this involved abstaining from alcohol and avoiding games of chance. The Church of Christ forbids musical instruments in worship; all music is a capella. A teacher in their seminary says, "Today we know there is really no theological or biblical justification for this, but it is our tradition." To adopt a tradition's unique practices binds us to a particular people's history and experience. We get a sense of this when the biblical Ruth declines to return to her people, their traditions, and beliefs, and says to her mother-in-law, Naomi, "Your people will be my people and your God my God" (Ruth 1:26b).

Viewing Tradition Through Digital Culture

Digital culture reimagines the role of tradition in shaping your religious identity and practice. There is less attention to the way shared habits and understandings connect you to a community. People feel free to shape how they interpret and use the religious stuff they inherit or appropriate.

While there is something distinctive about how individual our focus is today, it would be a mistake to see this as a break with an otherwise integrated Christian community. The variety of Christian expression is not a purely modern development. What we are learning about the early followers of Jesus and the rise of Christian communities reveals the diversity of Christian traditions. The New Testament description of the earliest Christian communities reveals their diversity and fervent debates about how to understand Jesus and his teaching and to live out Christian identity. There were different beliefs and practices among the earliest followers of Jesus, and Christian interpretations and practices continued to evolve over time. What we see today is an extension of that tradition of change.

Contemporary Christians are less likely to see tradition as an identity to be taken on in its entirety. Instead, it is a source of ideas and practices on which we draw. In considering what it means for us to be Christian, we pick and choose what beliefs to adopt and what practices to embody in our individually constructed Christian identities. Practical theologian Katherine Turpin suggests that people who rework and incorporate traditional practices and images may find authenticity in these elements of ancient traditions that they don't see in slick marketed new spiritual products.[5]

Digital culture encourages us to imagine tradition as a sort of data bank to be accessed, edited, and reused. The focus is on how individuals converse with, evaluate, and reform the tradition. The images, stories, and models for faithful action that have been handed down are potentially useful bytes of religious content to be appropriated and reused. A tradition is also seen as containing a residue of archaic cultural practices and understandings that can be discarded. When we see ourselves as digital constructions, tradition is a source of the bytes and pixels that can be incorporated in creative ways into the self we are writing. For those who think about religious identity in this way, it seems natural that Buddhist and Christian practices and assumptions might be treated as elements to be integrated into the self.

IDENTITY: INDIVIDUAL AND CONSTRUCTED

Writing about the current media age, Stewart Hoover observes that the central task of religion has become constructing and articulating an individual religious self.[6] Sometimes these constructions of identity are the result of intentional religious searching and self-conscious reflection. A colleague with adolescent children sees this as being like the way teens intentionally take on a style as a significant identity construction project, proclaiming "I am a Goth" or "I am a computer geek." We might think of someone who identifies as a Buddhist-Christian as an example of this sort of intentional religious identity construction.

There is also a lot of subtler accrual and mixing of religious meaning. When asked to describe her spiritual practice, a thirtysomething says, "Just . . . I do yoga, and my aunt sent me this statue of an angel when my baby was born, and I listen to praise music on the way to work." This disorganized assembly of identity, and the fact that it doesn't seem remarkable or need explanation, is evidence of how common this assemblage of religious practice and identity has become.

Identity Is Individual

Consider how the experience of digital technologies and the digital metaphor encourages people to think about religious identity in this personal way. Linguistically, *identity* is communal; the term asks a social question, "Who do you identify with?" Yet, today identity is seen as an individual project of meaning construction. Contemporary culture encourages you to hear questions about your identity as asking "Who are you?" not "Who are your people?" When we think in this way, we understand religious identity to be a matter of individual belief and practice. Faith traditions provide language and habits that help us name our religious questions and express religious identity. However, most people don't feel bound by the norms of any single tradition in the ways that they might once have. Obviously, this shift has implications for congregations and denominations.

Even if you identify with a particular denomination or tradition, you may have a complexly negotiated understanding of how you fit. You may claim the connection while nuancing church teachings you disagree with. For example, some people say, "I am Catholic, but don't follow the church's teaching on birth control." Or they locate themselves theologically or regionally within a particular strand of the tradition, saying, "I am a liberal Baptist" or "I am a southern Methodist."

Our relationship to tradition is complicated. It shapes you, even when you are not aware that this is happening. I think of people raised in evangelical homes who no longer attend evangelical churches yet remain thoroughly evangelical in worldview. Or former Catholics or non-observant Jews who sometimes more consciously claim their cultural Catholicism or Jewishness, even when it is not something they "believe" anymore. The contemporary assumption that identity is personal oversimplifies this. You and your children likely feel more freedom to sample and adapt tradition to fit your needs and less obligation to conform to tradition than did those who came before you. Clearly, many people are putting religious sources together in quite individualized and sometimes surprising ways. Yet, even as we pick and choose, there is a level at which exposure to tradition forms us.

This modern sense that identity is personal stands in stark contrast to the way communal cultures experience identity. In such societies people receive their religious identity from the community, and religion ties them to a particular people. The assumption that religious identity is a matter of family was explicit when the prophet Joshua calls on the gathered tribes to renew their covenant with the God of Israel and proclaims, "As for me and my household, we will follow the Lord" (Joshua 24:15 NRSV). In a society where identity comes from the group, the leader determines the religious identity of the community. Outside of certain fundamentalist communities, it is almost impossible for modern Americans to think about their own identity in this way.

It shouldn't surprise us that people who think in this highly individualized way don't assume that congregations are necessary elements in their spiritual lives. We must make a case for shared religion. Church consultant Tom Bandy discusses this transition from "institutionally structured religion" to a personalized religion that he describes as "contextually customized by lifestyle." Bandy sees congregations adapt to this by making increasing room for individual customization. For example, he notes that many congregations have stopped repeating the Apostles creed because it doesn't work for them to impose an assumed statement of shared beliefs.[7]

Identity Is Constructed within a Shared Community of Feeling

Today, people are less inclined to think of their religious identity as fixed. We think about what it means to be human through the digital metaphor. Because this way of thinking is so pervasive, we consciously or unconsciously think of our own identity, including our religious identity, as under constant reconstruction.

In the previous paragraph, the word "unconsciously" is significant. This talk of the construction of identity and of how digital culture encourages us to understand identity seems to suggest that people are constantly self-consciously measuring the adequacy of their religious identity. Most people don't carefully plan the next addition to their practice or articulate the theological assumptions inherent in their religious identity. While it is clear from the popularity of spiritual self-help books, workshops, blogs, and retreats that such people exist, they are the tip of the iceberg. Below the water are people who participate in "a shared community of feeling." While they are not consciously evaluating the adequacy of their religious identity, they are not surprised by other people's religious construction or resistant to their own attraction to new spiritual possibilities.

In digital culture this process of religious self-discovery does not need to be examined and articulated; it simply seems to be "the way it is." A beloved relative of mine, who is sustained by an evangelical practice, fills her house with angel figurines. I am not suggesting that when she buys them, she thinks, "This porcelain figure expresses my confidence in an interventionist God who is always watching over me and keeping me safe." Nor would it occur to her that displaying them is a "performance of her Christian identity." These acts of acquiring and displaying simply rest on shared and mostly unexamined assumptions about how the world works.

Today, it seems that the Christian life is a never-ending process of defining and performing religious identity. This performance can seem indulgent to those who assume that faithful Christian action grows out of firmly established identity. For them, the right practice grows out of the correct belief. However, in many contemporary Christian communities, belief and identity are worked out along the way. For instance, the opportunity to do something for and with people without homes is often what attracts people to *After Hours, Denver*. Later, concepts from the Christian story become a way to think about this work, about the lives of these neighbors without homes, and about the volunteers' own lives. Both for those served and those serving, participation creates a space to ponder, clarify, and practice their own religious identities. For them, theology grows out of practice.

CONSTRUCTION: ADOPTION, HYPHENATION, SAMPLING, AND MASHUP

How do people construct religious identity? They do not create it out of nothing. To be sure, many people continue the practice of *adoption*, either of their parents' religion or that of other significant people in their lives. Drawing on the digital metaphor and hip-hop culture for analogies, three alternative processes are becoming more common today, *hyphenation*, *sampling*, and *mashup*.

Adoption

Adoption is the way that people traditionally acquired religious identity. It was hardly a matter of conscious decision. If you were raised in a religious family, you adopted the religion into which they are born. You might better say you were adopted by the religion than that you consciously adopted the faith. Modernity and the rise of the individual made religion a more private matter, and exposure to a broader range of practice made people more aware of their religious options. But even with choice, most religious people largely adopted one established religion or another.

In discussing changes in how Americans relate to religion, it is easy to imagine that in the past everyone was religious and involved with organized religion and observe that now they are not. Historians suggest that the pattern is more complicated. There were ups and downs; for instance, before a wave of Protestant revivals in the early nineteenth century, only about 20 percent of Americans were involved in organized religion. After this "Second Great Awakening," religious participation peaked as high as 80 percent before dropping off again.[8] After World War II, soldiers returned and took up family life. This was another period when organized religion grew. Today, people often see the postwar era as the norm and treat the decline of organized religion that began later in the twentieth century as an aberration. It is probably more accurate to think that in every era, there were those for whom the practice of religion was central to their identity, other occasional and perhaps reluctant participants, and people who gave religion little thought.

That is not to say that the current decline in organized religion is not a significant challenge for congregations. It has extended over several generations. Thus, many people do not have a "born into" tradition to accept or reject. Even those who expose their children to a particular form of religious life often express a desire for the child to choose their spiritual path. And, as we have already seen, people who do adopt a religious tradition are less likely to think of it as something that must be embraced in its entirety.

Hyphenation

Hyphenation suggests the linking of distinct traditions, often signaled typographically with a hyphen. Anglo-Catholics use the hyphen to signal that their Episcopal (or Anglo) identity is simultaneously Catholic. A Christian-Buddhist simultaneously practices Buddhism and Christianity.[9] The individual embraces both traditions, neither tradition is subsumed into the other, and the individual serves as the link between them. For the practitioner, participation in one cannot be understood without acknowledging the other.

Sampling

Digital technologies make it easy to edit music, lift a musical phrase or lyric out of one recording and incorporate it in another. *Sampling* is a creative practice in which hip-hop artists borrow a section from someone's work and incorporate it into a new aesthetic context. Often this gives the passage new meaning that grows out of the way it is juxtaposed with other music elements.

In a similar sense, people sample a religion, choosing an element to integrate into their own religious identity. Not every Christian who flies Buddhist prayer flags is a Buddhist-Christian. Some people sampled an element of Buddhist practice and integrated it into a predominantly Christian identity. Similarly, someone who doesn't have any regular Christian practice but who puts up a manger scene in December might be thought of as sampling Christianity.

Sampling often happens within the Christian tradition. Some people who primarily identify as Protestant collect and meditate on Orthodox icons or read the daily meditation posted online by the Franciscan priest Father Richard Rohr. Similarly, some Catholics attend evangelical Bible studies. Each understands her or himself as located within a tradition but feels free to draw on, or sample, another.

Mashup

Mashup is another term from hip-hop culture. Here there is less sense of one primary identity sampling another. Instead, a unique creation integrates elements from different sources. For example, *The Grey Album* by DJ Danger Mouse is a mashup of the Rapper Jay-Z's *The Black Album* with samples from the Beatles untitled collection known as the "White Album." The play continues as other artists parody, sample, or otherwise rework the original mashup.

In studying how popular music does theological work, John S. McClure explores the way new theological ideas are created through the mashup of tradition with new ideas and contexts.[10] I extend the idea of mashup to describe the religious identity constructions of people who sample and combine without having a clear home base in any single tradition. They are neither hyphenating two traditions that remain distinct nor sampling a practice, image, or concept from one faith system to integrate into another. The self is the center for the mashup artist, who combines elements from various traditions in a unique religious mashup. One place we see this happening is among people who think of themselves as "spiritual but not religious." They gather from varied religious resources, putting things together in unique and creative ways.

CONSUMING RELIGION

I try to avoid suggesting a hierarchy between (1) material religion, such as sanctuaries, art, and religious clothing; (2) practices like receiving communion, crossing oneself, or saying, "God bless you"; and (3) theological ideas about God, persons, and the world. I resist the assumption that doctrines are the core of the faith, and that images, objects, and practices merely express these claims. Rather, theologies and doctrines are our effort to talk about what Morgan called religion's "pervasive community of feeling" that produces "the felt expectation that the world works in a particular way."[11]

What happens when people acquire religious symbols and objects is complicated. Does possession of a religion's material expressions, such as Buddhist prayer flags or a tattoo of a religious text or image, give us access to the spiritual worlds from which they come? Or is the life of feelings and sensations out of which they came more difficult to access? Critics of consumption argue that this often-casual collection of religious images and objects lacks substance. It involves little more than acquiring and re-presenting concepts, language, techniques, and material by people who fail to comprehend the religious systems they are sampling. In short, it is merely a form of consumption without religious meaning.

That may often be true, but it is worth considering the counterargument. Perhaps you can consume religion. The objects and images you surround yourselves with say something about you. Since this consumption of religion seems prolific today, we should try to understand it.

Religious consumption is hardly a new phenomenon. Crusaders carried what they understood to be relics of the early church back to Europe, where cathedrals and museums preserve them to this day. Later generations of travelers to Israel/Palestine buy vials of water from the Jordan and Armenian pottery. They hope the objects will evoke the sensations and spiritual histories of the places they visited. It is not easy to separate our religious motivations from other desires. This confusion of desires was true of the crusaders, and today it remains hard to separate the tourist's motivation to visit exotic places from the pilgrim's thirst for spiritual sensations.

Some Critiques of Consumption

Today's culture of consumption raises significant social and theological concerns. People are encouraged to think of things they can buy—such as clothes, cars, or electronic gear—as expressions of status. Our choices are driven by an advertising system that promises satisfactions that the goods cannot deliver. Ethical questions are raised by the conditions of the workers who produce what we buy and the impact of production on the environment. Thus, the consumptive approach to identity can be a shallow distraction from the spiritual path to religious identity that comes through service and reflection.

Consumption meshes with the American focus on the individual. People who place a high value on autonomy feel free to acquire objects, ideas, and practices and use them as they wish. We are not inclined to ask what the effect might be on the traditions we are consuming. This is particularly troubling when people from dominant communities appropriate the traditions of communities who lack the cultural standing and capital to resist. My colleague "Tink" Tinker, a member of the Osage Nation, taught generations of students to be suspicious of the way some white folks consume, or he would say "appropriate," native practices such as that of the sweat lodge or honoring the four directions. Too often, this happens without understanding the broader cultural experience and worldview out of which they come.[12]

Just as we acquire physical stuff that expresses religious identity, people absorb concepts and practices from the religion that surrounds them. For instance, individuals and communities from minority traditions often unintentionally consume the religious language, ideas, and bodily expressions of the religious majority in their region. In a Baptist region, everyone's religious life is a little bit Baptist. It is also the case that when people adopt the dominant religion, they bring with them elements and assumptions from their previous practice; in Afro-Brazil, everyone's Catholicism is a little bit African.

In digital culture, identity construction seems tied to consumption. Can we take these critiques of consumption seriously while at the same time reframing how we think about consumption and the people who seem to find their religious identity in the things they consume? Are there positive aspects to the consumption of an object like an orthodox icon, a statue of the Hindu god Ganesh, or a religious action like pilgrimage or foot washing?

A common critique of consumption is that the consumer's satisfaction is not in the object—or the tradition it comes out of—but in the act of consumption, therefore the consumer must continue to acquire. If the folks we are discussing are doing more than that, if the consumption is part of constructive projects that extend their religious identities, then these acts of acquisition seem more substantive. It does leave unaddressed the question of what it cost the source tradition.

Reframing Consumption

Theologian Vincent Miller suggests that "the positive potential of . . . consumer culture must be taken seriously. . . . It constructs every person as the author of his or her identity."[13] For Miller, this potential for consumers to construct rather than passively adopt identity rests on two things we have been discussing. First, contemporary culture provides consumers with a wide array of stories and products through which they express themselves. Secondly, digital technologies make it easier for everyday people to consume, produce, and share. People blog and tweet, post memes and graffiti, and rework in various ways the stories and products they consume.

In a culture where so many products are available, it is difficult to choose among them. Whether you are "shopping" for toothpaste or religious practices, the sheer range of possibilities is overwhelming. People have adopted the term *curation* from museums and art galleries to describe this process of selecting and combining elements so that together they make a statement. Individuals thus curate the religious material, practices, and assumptions they gather to express personal religious identity.

To take a secular example, think of the statement made when a woman wears a sundress with a pair of Doc Martens. The combination creates an entirely different expression about her femininity and strength than either of the products alone. This mixing of elements can be a sort of mindful consumption in which things point to more profound articulations of identity. Similarly, such meaningful construction can be going on in the lives of those who hyphenate, sample, or mashup elements from different religious traditions. Congregations and religious leaders rooted in those traditions are often uncomfortable with those who draw on their tradition without fully embracing it. Yet there is an opportunity for those who know these traditions to help individuals think more deeply about their constructed religious identities and the sources from which they consume that can build networks of connection.

Paying attention to contemporary Christian life in consumer culture demonstrates that not all consumption is passive. People acquire and curate images, ideas, and material expressions from various religious sources and, through acts of religious imagination, combine them in new ways. By taking the authority to author their own identity, they challenge established religious systems that seek to tell people who they are. There is undoubtedly a strong pushback from religious and societal structures. Yet it is not easy to control folks who claim the freedom to pick and choose, to reimagine their stories.

To be clear, this desire to clarify, articulate, and live out religious identity is not something that is only happening outside congregations. It is already at work in people within established communities of faith. Congregations that recognize and befriend this desire can articulate the larger logic and wisdom of their tradition, bring people together to envision new ways of ministry, and produce new forms of Christian community.

PERFORMING IDENTITY

In social media everyone is a performer. Technology makes digital construction easy. With downloadable programs and just a little expertise, one can shoot and edit a movie on an iPhone or synthesize music on a laptop. What people construct, whether art or identity itself, is performed. Almost anyone can have a website or blog where they express themselves. Of course, this performance of identity also happens offline. Acts of consumption, such as the purchase of a Black Lives Matter hoody or a pro-gun bumper sticker, involve more than acquiring messages about public issues. They are also statements about us and our commitments; this is especially true when these items are modified, curated, or combined with other material in more complex individual performances.

The performance of religious identity can involve wearing distinctive garb like the yarmulke with which some Jewish men cover their heads or the once popular "What would Jesus do?" T-shirts. People might perform their identity by attending some religiously themed movies or boycotting others. Identity is created and performed through many expressive daily habits. They can be quite simple. When a Muslim says, *"inshallah,"* which means "God willing," or a Christian says, "God bless you," they are performing their identity.

Identity is also explored and expressed in peak experiences that may not be repeated but continue to have meaning for the performer. One example of this is the practice of walking the *Camino* (road) *de Santiago* in Spain. The account of a shepherd's vision of "a great light" made Santiago a pilgrimage site, and walking the road became a common spiritual practice rooted in medieval times. Though it fell out of favor for a time, the pilgrimage has reemerged, and not only among Catholics. Walking the entire modern route can take a month or more.

A Protestant that I know traveled to Spain to walk a portion of the *Camino*. His is not a medieval Catholic spirituality. He is unlikely to repeat the walk. Yet, he reports that his temporary adoption of the pilgrim's discipline on the road to Santiago created a space to explore and deepen his Christian identity. The experience of having been a walker of the *Camino* remains a shaping experience in his understanding and expression of his identity as a Christian.

It is too simple to describe the relationship between the construction and performance of religious identity in linear terms. It is not that we first construct an identity and then perform it. Often people work out an identity in action. At church camp and service projects, people try on practices or aspects of Christian identity. Something similar happens when people buy a book on religion or spirituality, go on pilgrimages, or attend a retreat. Like a Wikipedia essay that is forever subject to editing, the religious self is never finalized. The bodily memory practice elicits lives on; the practitioner combines it with new experiences in the ongoing search for a rich and satisfying religious self.

If you care about congregations and want to build relevant forms of Christian community, what are you to make of this individually focused spirituality? Once we thought of our Christian identity as fixed. Such religious identity came from adopting and being adopted by a particular faith tradition. To say one was Baptist or Buddhist, Muslim or Methodist, was to take identity from the community.

Today, people don't so easily conform to religious institutions. When identity is personal, congregations do not seem essential. People see our faith traditions as collections of resources that they can draw on rather than as authoritative models to which they should conform. Those who describe their constructed identity as "spiritual but not religious" question whether organized and institutional forms of religion are worth the effort.

Frankly, many who stay involved in congregational life have similar questions. Though we may love our congregations, we know that they can be exclusionary, rigid, and resistant to change. We joke about the battles fought over weighty matters such as changing the hour of services or the carpet color. Yet we know that our focus on these things diverts us from helping people find the language, concepts, and tools that help them grasp God or be grasped by God.

In a world where it is not self-evident that the only or best place to live out a Christian life is within a congregation, churches must demonstrate that they are useful to people who want to grasp God, construct a religious identity, and live faithfully. Someone I used to worship with said, "I want my church to accept me as I am and invite me to be more." To be able to invite the people we worship with—and people outside the church who also have spiritual questions and gifts—to be more, we have first to accept them as they are.

Today that means accepting that many people see the construction of their religious identity as an ongoing task. They may not know much about your faith tradition or give much authority to it. They are likely to assume that religion is something to be consumed and reconstructed. They will only be interested in participating in congregational life to the extent that it serves their religious journey. I hope that congregations engaged with the gospel will help each of us be more than we have been. However, our acceptance of those exploring and constructing religious identity cannot be conditional. We won't be useful to them if our claim to "accept them as they are" rests on the assumption that we know what they will become. It is hard and humbling to accept that others will construct new forms of Christian identity, practice, and community. Yet, that is our calling.

DISCUSSION QUESTIONS

- Do you see your own religious identity as something you have inherited from family or tradition? What has been helpful or challenging about that?
- Do you see your religious identity as something that you constructed from multiple sources? What sources do you draw on?

- Describe a significant or meaningful practice in your faith community. How is it tied to tradition? How is it not?
- Give examples of individuals' religious *adoption, hyphenation, sampling*, and *mashup* from your own experience and observation.
- What are some positive and negative examples of religious consumption?

4

Connections in Communities and Networks

Seeking out brothers, and sisters, and mothers . . .

The previous chapter examined the modern tendency to see identity—including religious identity—as an individual project. That turn to the personal is one reason for the statistical decline in congregational membership and participation and the increase in the number of people who reply "none" when asked to identify with a religious community. This chapter examines the rise of networks of communication and relationship, considers how congregations are affected by those changes, and explores new forms of networked faith community that are emerging.

A few key ideas shape this discussion:

- Fewer people are involved in organized religion and many congregations have closed their doors. Anxiety about this produces nostalgia for an idealized past in which families, communities, and congregations changed little over generations. This nostalgia makes it harder to respond to the fluidity of the present day.
- The image of *fluid networks*, used to describe how information flows in digital communications, helps us think about how people relate today. These networks lack the clear center, often around a leader or shared identity, characteristic of traditional communities. Instead, each person is the center of their own network of relationships.
- The network is less stable than the traditional community. Here, people relatively easily launch new relationships and let others go in a constantly changing web of connection.

- These changes invite new models of congregation, connection, and caring, and new ways of working with and for those wounded by society.

People today think about religious identity as a deeply personal project. For many, the practice of faith is not rooted in a relationship with a particular tradition, denomination, or congregation. At least in part, this is what is meant by the suggestion that people are "spiritual but not religious."

Some people see this as the end of congregations. Though congregations face unique challenges today, I don't think that is inevitable. I do believe that many congregations are wedded to structures, patterns of relating, and forms of expression that make little sense in digital culture. If you think that is correct, you should consider whether the way your congregation gathers for worship and mutual support and organizes itself attracts others and makes good news clear in a changing world. Not everything we preserve from the church's past continues to be life giving, and there will be tension between improving what exists and creating something new as we live into digital culture.

WHY CONGREGATIONS?

Is church worth the effort, particularly in the messy expensive form of its institutional life? Former religion professor, author, and public speaker Barbara Brown Taylor served as an Episcopal priest. She describes the "loss of faith" that the institutional church continues to provide "right language, concepts, and tools to grasp God,"[1] which lead her to give up that work. Today, many people who describe themselves as "spiritual but not religious," apparently indicating that they too have lost confidence that organized religion adds enough value to spiritual practice to be worth the effort.

Too often, congregations seem bound up in forms of institutional maintenance that their critics dismiss as turf battles over who picks the color of the carpet. Using the lens of media and mediation, *Church as Network* seeks to help existing congregations find the "language, concepts, and tools" that help people form religious identities and connections that are worth the effort because they point us to what Brown Taylor elsewhere calls "the Real Thing."

Practical theologian Pete Ward suggests that, in a world shaped by movement and change, Christians must give up their longing for stability. He believes that nostalgia is producing congregations that are museums dedicated to a dying way of life. Ward calls on Christians to move beyond what he calls the "solid Church" of the past to make ready for the rise of a "fluid Church"[2] that can adapt to a networked culture. In such a society, congregations that seek to connect us with God and other people need to figure out how to create and maintain faith communities that welcome, connect with, and say goodbye to a stream of people.

The idea of social networks first emerged to explain how highly mobile people relate. In America, people move often, may not know their neighbors, and don't easily join organizations. If they seek a faith community, they must find one with each move and establish new relationships. That can be exhausting, particularly if they don't find congregations welcoming. Many eventually give up.

Mobility also requires congregations to think in new ways about how they relate to their neighborhoods. I think of a parish in a bustling northside Chicago neighborhood full of young adults launching their careers. On average they change jobs, marry distant loved ones, leave for graduate school, or otherwise move on every four to five years. Just to keep up, this congregation must take in more than 20 percent of their membership every year. Doing this requires them to envision community differently, be more welcoming, and do a better job of incorporating new folks. While not all communities face that rate of turnover, the congregation illustrates a pattern.

One reason that it is harder than it once was for congregations to replace the folks they lose is that the pool of people seeking organized religious communities is shrinking. Today many people "reject conventional religious affiliation, while not giving up their religious feelings."[3] Gallup Polls reports that church membership and attendance have been falling since the 1970s and have plunged 20 percent in the last two decades. Thus, "thousands of U.S. churches close each year."[4] Increasingly congregations are competing to attract participants from a shrinking pool.

These changes are disheartening. Congregations who don't pay attention to how mobility affects their community, who ignore the decline of organized religion, and who don't take note of the rise of social networks are likely to see their own decline in membership and the increased inward focus that often follows, as evidence of an individual failing. Understanding these changes as part of a broader shift in culture, in which old forms of community are being replaced by looser networks of connection, can help us understand the decline and envision the sort of fluid church that Ward calls for.

What are the implications of networks for congregational life? Networks are open and easily reconfigure around new people. They ask less of those coming in the door yet invite their voices. Connecting with a religious network is not a marriage or adoption. In social media terms, you only need to "like" the congregation or leader. This makes it easier to take relational risks. Of course, it is also easy to pull back from the relationship or to leave the network, to "unfriend" the congregation or faith leader. To make sense of these changes, and build networks of relationship, caring congregations must better understand how those fluid connections are built, maintained, and experienced in digital culture.

COMMUNITY

According to Merriam-Webster, a community is a "unified body of individuals" with "common interests . . . characteristics . . . history . . . [or] socioeconomic conditions."[5] Yet, when we long for community, we mean more than simply people with something in common. Later, in exploring the term, the dictionary says "fellowship." That begins to capture the sense of Christian community as a place where we feel known, cared for, and called to work together to build a better world.

To picture how community is changing, some people who study social relationships contrast traditional communities with fluid social networks. Some speak as though we must be one or the other. I think it is more accurate to think of a continuum of models of communities that range from fairly fixed and unchanging "traditional" communities to more fluid "network" communities. Below, I will describe the two ends of the spectrum. You will likely locate your congregation somewhere on the continuum between them.

Traditional Community

Here community exists between people whose identity and relationships are homogeneous, relatively fixed, and organized around a leader. Members often belong to the same social class or race and share assumptions about the roles of women and men in the family and community. They don't think of their practice of faith, and the theologies and values it rest on, as choices but as the natural structure of the church. They have what sociologists call a *habitus*,[6] a set of shared mannerisms, tastes, moral intentions, and habits through which they interpret their experience. New people enter slowly since they must adopt the *habitus* before they are fully accepted and invited to take leadership.

The pastor of a small Methodist parish in a stable Chicago neighborhood recalls this example of such traditional community. The neighborhood was experiencing racial change. The congregation was losing longtime members as older people died or move to be closer to family in the suburbs. The elderly white congregants were not attracting the younger Black and Latinx families moving into the community. Those who visited did not become regular participants. To describe the way fixed patterns of relationship make change hard, the pastor uses this example. Women in the congregation were invited to join social and service groups called "circles." One is the *Young Married Circle*. However, the membership of that circle was made of women in their seventies and eighties, most of them widows.

This is such a poignant story. It captures both the richness of traditional communities and why change is difficult for them. Most of the women in the *Young Married Circle* had been participating for fifty or more years. They raised children, worked for mission, and buried husbands together. What a lovely legacy of caring Christian relationships! At the same time, imagine being a young woman of color who responds to the announcement that the circle is meeting. The group doesn't deliver on what it promises about the age, marital status, and life issues of its membership. Should the visitor still want to participate, she must break into long-established relationships and tease out the habits and attitudes shared by insiders. If the circle is a picture of the congregation, we see immediately why insiders love it dearly and why it doesn't feel welcoming to new folks.

We can think of these traditional religious communities through the image of a wheel. They are organized around a *hub,* which might be a particular leader or religious identity. Typically, in a small congregation like the one described above, that leader is not the pastor. Pastors come and go; the leader is a long-standing and influential layperson. The person at the hub is the one who articulates the community's identity, organizes and disciplines, and teaches the community's habits and practices.

People, represented as *spokes* in our image, are connected to that hub by their often-unexamined adoption of practices of the congregation. The wheel also has a rim that marks the community's outer limit; there are insiders and outsiders. Such congregations are particularly good at conserving their heritage, habits, skills and dispositions, and existing relationships. Insiders are sustained by lasting relationships; they feel known and cared for. Because their religious identity is rooted in the congregation, they are prepared to make sacrifices and give generously of their time and money.

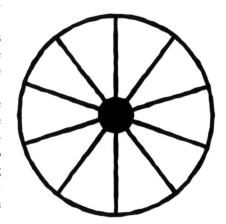

Perhaps our most romantic image of traditional community is the nuclear family. Often, smaller congregations turn to this metaphor to describe their experience of being deeply formed, known, and cared for. But experiencing the congregation as family underscores its difficulty in responding to significant change. For insiders, the family church's expectations are clear, and the norms and habits of the community deeply ingrained. They don't have to be discussed. This clarity about roles, behaviors, and relationships strengthens connections between insiders; yet what makes the congregation seem warm and caring to members of the family signals to newcomers that it is going to be hard to break in.

Change makes a traditional community's *habitus* visible. It can raise questions about whether they have the right hub and break down the boundaries that tell members who belongs and who doesn't. This requires them to build connections with people who don't share their habits and attitudes. Since the existing structures of the congregation are aligned with certain people's self-interest, these changes raise anxieties that can deepen the resistance to new people and practices. Sometimes, this is petty. My spouse and I were just getting settled into a pew in a congregation we were visiting when a woman approached and said, "You are in my seat." She is not alone in communicating "This is my church, nothing should happen that disrupts me."

Movement and fluidity bring in people who do not share our habits and assumptions. They may come from different social classes and have different racial and ethnic identities, sexual orientations, or theologies. The desire to live in an idealized past blunts the radical welcome of the foreign and different that Jesus modeled. A man in a predominantly white congregation in a racially changing neighborhood once told me, only half-jokingly, "We want more people like us, but younger, who will support the church like we have done, without making any changes." The resistance to change produces a nostalgic vision of the congregation that masks both the challenges and possibilities the congregation faces. Thus, the resistant community has difficulty imagining a different future for itself.

Real change requires the hard work of questioning and altering power relationships. The image of the networked community, discussed below, provides a way to think about realigning relationships that welcomes new people and responds to their needs and interests. However, it is naïve to think that people easily give up power, or that power isn't at work in our networked relationships.

Networked Community

At the other end of the spectrum from the largely fixed and long-lasting community is the loose network. It is always in motion. In a network there is no center; people participate in multiple overlapping groups. Rather than taking their identity from a single primary community, identity is worked out in often-shifting connections. Media scholar Heidi Campbell writes, "The network image helps us examine the complex interplay and negotiations occurring between individuals and the community, new and old sources of authority, and public and private identities."[7] Here even people who belong to a particular congregation and identify with a particular tradition often think of these as significant locations in a wider and fluid religious network that helps to shape their identity.

The term "network" describes both the way computers and the internet link communications systems and a kind of social relationship that might exist on- or offline. Social media highlight and encourage this networked way of thinking about relationships. As early as the late 1960s and early 1970s, sociologists, seeking new ways to understand community, developed "social network analysis." They noticed that our metaphors for community were largely geographic. People imagined neighborhoods or towns gathered around a public square where people settled, and everyone was known by their neighbors. If they considered religion, they imagined it organized in stable parishes like the village congregation disrupted by the arrival of a new and female priest in the British comedy *The Vicar of Dibley*.

Network analysis asks what friendship and community look like when impersonal strip malls replace the town square. Thinking about social structures and connections rather than spaces and places also draws attention to the ways that people relate within digital culture.[8] This approach helps us see the challenges and possibilities congregations face today. It is not just that some forms of religion have moved online, as when *After Hours, Denver* followers organize and pray online or congregations hold virtual worship services during the COVID-19 pandemic. The logic of networked relationships shapes the way we relate to congregations whether we practice our faith online or offline.

WHAT MEDIA TEACHES US ABOUT NETWORKS

Sociologist Manuel Castells suggests that we no longer live in an industrial age, but rather in an information age.[9] Using an electronic analogy, Castells says that the network is an information system made up of linked nodes (people, organizations, communications systems, and political structures). Rather than seeing a community as a wheel with little interaction between the spokes and information flowing out from the leader to followers, the network is a spiderweb with a node at each intersection.

Here, information and relationship flow from node to node. Everyone is both a sender and receiver of information. We saw, in the discussion of identity construction, how individuals drew on multiple sources to construct a religious self. While we, and the algorithms that manage digital information, make choices about who we seek information from and who we share it with, there is no clear boundary. There is no rim to the wheel. The web of information keeps shifting and expanding. A web of relationships is similarly fluid.

The image of the spiderweb helps us see that in the network, information flows in every direction, but it still looks like it has a center. In fact, each node is itself the center of a web of relationships. Here another image is helpful. A Venn diagram is a series of overlapping circles that seeks to capture the complexity of our relationships, helps us imagine the flow of information and relationship in the web.

Facebook illustrates this. I am part of a series of groups that overlap on my Facebook page. My circles include, my extended family, people in my congregation, professional colleagues interested in the relationships of religion, media, and culture, my social acquaintances, people I connect with through my work on immigration issues, and folks I ride bicycles with. In pre-network models of community, these circles are kept separate, each is allowed to imagine that it is my primary location. In some places I live out my role in my family, in other places I am a member of my religious community, and in others I present a professional self to colleagues and students. In contrast, on Facebook all these people are my "friends," and they see each other as they respond to my posts, and I see them and their friends.

Here is one example of how a networked digital connection brings people together. One morning, I was startled to learn from a stranger's Facebook post that a dear friend had experienced a massive heart attack and died. Michael was a writer and poet, a denominational executive, a pastor with a national reputation as a storyteller, and a friend, husband, and father. In the days following his death, his Facebook page filled with hundreds of posts by those who had known him in these various contexts. People expressed their sense of loss, posted pictures, told stories about things he had done, what he had taught us, and about what his life meant to us. We commented on each other's posts and prayed for each other and Michael's wife and daughters.

In a digital space, former parishioners, folks from the storytelling network, people who knew his poetry, and past and present friends and colleagues came together to mourn, celebrate, and remember. This activity was intense for a few weeks, and then largely trailed off. Then on his birthday there was a brief flurry of further remembrances. For a period, Michael's Facebook page was the triangle in the middle of the Venn diagram, the space where his overlapping communities connected. Without him, our paths may not cross again. Yet we were able to share our grief, listen to each other's stories, and support one another in our loss.

Such experiences illustrate the complexity and fluidity of networked relationships. Where the traditional community focuses attention on a single set of relationships such as a neighborhood, an ethnic identity, or a local faith community, the network envisions multiple overlapping communities or hubs of connection. Here everyone is the hub of a web of evolving relationships, some of them long-standing and others ephemeral.

SOME LIMITATIONS OF DIGITAL COMMUNICATION AND NETWORKED RELATIONSHIPS

Just as the traditional community can be criticized for romanticizing stable hierarchical relationships, it is easy to romanticize the networks that seem to make it possible to connect with anyone. For some critics, brief online gatherings—while they may be intense at the time—ought not to be equated with sustained face-to-face connections like those of the congregation who gathered in a physical sanctuary for Michael's funeral and who brought meals to his family. Just as we did in thinking about traditional communities, we should think carefully about both the possibilities that networks offer and their limitations and challenges.

Networks Are Not as Open as They Seem

While it is tempting to imagine the network as a world of infinite possibility, Castells warns that the information doesn't flow entirely freely through the web. There are what he calls "switches" that control the flow of information.

The algorithms that shape Google, Facebook and other online systems are digital switches. Based on our past likes and existing relationships, they switch certain information toward us and other information away. The people who are nodes in our networks function similarly.

The suggestion that Facebook is a network of "friends" masks the way that social media mines and sells your data. To build markets for advertisers, social media drives you toward people who match your demographic, and share your opinions and social location. Because the algorithms pick up society's unexamined assumptions about race and gender, seemingly blind searches often exclude persons of color and women.[10] Ironically, the very technologies that make it possible for us to build links across theological, geographical, and social differences confirm our biases and point us toward those who share our assumptions and prejudices.

Our own choices also drive us toward people who share our interests and biases. We follow people we find interesting, and block or unfriend those who offend. You can work against these tendencies to build networks that confirm your prejudices. However, this takes vigilance. It requires active engagement to seek out a network that includes people from different social locations who thoughtfully challenge our preconceptions.

How does understanding this help you think about your congregation, its vision of the church, and its ministry? In digital culture, the flow of information is massive. Since no one can engage it all, the choices we make to manage the flow, and the way the system of algorithms makes these choices for us, shape the way we image our local community and its relationship to wider worlds, how we think about ourselves and others, and how we understand God and what it means to follow Jesus. These choices provide the images, ideas, materials, and feelings we work with as we construct personal and shared identities and practices.

Strong and Weak Ties

The suggestion that networks and online relationships lack depth was noted above. The relationships established online may not last. The content of the communication may be trivial or designed to confirm our existing attitudes. Certainly, reposting a story about Black Lives Matter, or putting a BLM poster up outside the church building, is hardly the same as building deep relationships and working to transform your community. This criticism questions whether networks and digital spaces can support strong ties, assumes that weak ties don't matter, and asks whether these ways of connecting can deepen Christian practice and advance the life of congregations.

Memoirist and religion professor Deanna Thompson responds by discussing strong and weak tie relationships.[11] Strong ties are intense, certain, and reliable. However, they require significant energy and attention; people can maintain only a limited number of strong-tie relationships. As an illustration of their importance, Thompson describes what strong social ties meant to her when cancer made her dependent on others. Yet she also notes that sociologists tell us that relationships are established and maintained by both strong and weak ties. Think of the way that social courtesies establish weak but real connections in neighborhoods and congregations. You say "good morning" to neighbors whose names you don't know, point a visitor to the Sunday School, or ask an acquaintance, "How are you?" Deeper relationships often rest on these weaker connections. Thompson found that in addition to the strong ties with family and close friends that provided regular spiritual and material support she took comfort from a wider web of folks with whom she had weaker ties. They followed her illness and recovery online, inquired after her, prayed occasionally, and sent good wishes.

Thompson uses the emergence of the Black Lives Matter movement as an example of the way weak-tie connections can become strong and online connection can lead to face-to-face relationships. The phrase Black Lives Matter was launched in a widely shared online post. That led to often weak-tie social media conversations. Those discussions encouraged face-to-face conversation among people who eventually built stronger social ties. Together those discussions generated public protest and negotiation with police and civic leaders. Congregations that see the value of having a range of strong and weak relationships should build a web of weak but welcoming relationships, encouraging the places where those contacts invite stronger connection and engagement.

Embracing Fleeting Moments of Church

The desire to maintain institutions keeps congregations focused on long-term relationships. This can blind us to rich parts of the Christian experience that are more transitory. Revivals, retreats, pilgrimages, and church camp create intense peak experiences. Such brief, ephemeral, spiritual experiences make sense to a fluid culture. In fact, while fewer people in our fluid culture seem to want the weekly discipline of congregational worship, folks are hungry for the opportunity to come together for deep spiritual moments and to ritualize times of mourning or celebration. Congregations miss significant opportunities if they ignore these opportunities to connect with others.

During the week that my friend Michael was being memorialized on Facebook, another tragedy brought a wider network of people together. In the aftermath of school shootings in Parkland, Florida,[12] young people across the country organized the "March for Our Lives" in Washington, DC, and other communities across the country. They had been using sites like Twitter, Instagram, and Tumblr to mourn and reflect on the Parkland deaths and the larger issue of gun violence in America. They also used social media to organize. They called on students to march and talk to legislators, and on adults to act to make a change. It wasn't in a narrow sense a religious event, though the movement has spiritual elements. Some of their actions may have been cathartic but transitory. Or we may be seeing the forging of ongoing relationships out of which a movement for social change will come.

Communal celebration and mourning are regular locations of public religion today. In such gatherings people who may identify as spiritual, but not be part of established faith communities, come together without clear structures or formal religious leaders. We see this in the rituals that arise in response to both public and private tragedies or at times of awe. A cross erected at the site of a tragic traffic accident, flowers and teddy bears left where a child died, or a hundred thousand people gathering in Central Park after John Lennon's murder. More joyously, tourists gather at Stonehenge for the solstice, friends gather for a wedding, you watch a sunset, or come upon a drum circle in the park and are—sometimes—touched by the sacred. In slightly more organized and extended ways, people also seek out short-term religious experiences. They show up in congregations on Christmas and Easter, attend retreats, or take classes. A Trappist monastery in South Caroline advertises that "monastic guests" can be a monk for a month.[13]

Existing and emerging congregations might keep these gatherings in mind as they ponder Ward's notion of "[c]hurch as a series of relationships and communications." If our goal is institutional survival, they may seem a distraction. However, if our goal is to respond to the spiritual hunger of communities, then what congregations know about ritual, and about how to speak of the sacred in times of both loss and elation, may have something to offer. Can congregations become nodes that help organize and connect people into networks of religious significance? If so, some of those who gather at times of tragedy or celebration may be drawn to more lasting connections with established faith communities.

Access Is Not Universal

Another concern is that the technology that makes networked relationships ubiquitous is not universally available. Even if social media can help build meaningful community, some people live in places that do not have the consistent high-speed internet access that it requires. Others cannot afford the costs or choose not to participate in the systems that are available to them. We saw the consequence of this uneven distribution of digital resources when the COVID-19 pandemic drove schools online.

To be clear, people who lack or resist the technologies of networked communication still participate in a culture shaped by networked thinking. The network as metaphor remains a helpful way to think about the flow of information and relationships even in many places where the technologies of the digital network are not fully available. Still, though more and more people have internet access, congregations need to think about who they seek to serve and how to be accessible to those who do not have computers and the internet. The geographic and social location of the congregation will shape what is expected, possible, and appropriate.

Living into Change

Above, several cautions about digital technology and culture were considered: people have different levels of technical skill and access to technologies, the technologies can confirm our biases and exclude people that challenge our assumptions, networked relationships may be brief and lack depth. It may be tempting to imagine that we can avoid these challenges by clinging to old models of communications and assumptions about the nature of a community. However, as we have seen, traditional forms of community also have limits. Neither change, nor resistance to change, is without risks. Some current models of congregation will not be sustainable and not all the experiments with new ways of being church will be successful.

If the traditional family's strong ties and firm boundaries make it a particularly challenging model for community in times of change, perhaps emerging ways of thinking about the family could help us think about alternative forms of congregations. Where the family once seemed a primary unchanging community united by biology and structured by patriarchal authority, today people expect to negotiate the boundaries of their family. They may claim as family people to whom they are not related by blood and with whom they don't live. Though it can be unsettling, this is not an entirely new way of seeing the family. Jesus gets at this revisioning of what family might mean,

> While he was still speaking to the crowds, his mother and his brothers were standing outside, wanting to speak to him. Someone told him, "Look, your mother and your brothers are standing outside, wanting to speak to you." But to the one who had told him this, Jesus replied, "Who is my mother, and who are my brothers? And pointing to his disciples, he said, "Here are my mother and my brothers! For whoever does the will of my Father in heaven is my brother and sister and mother." (Matt. 12: 46–50 NRSV)

Congregations, at their best, provide opportunities for human connection and caring that unites people with each other and with God. They share a story that make a change in their communities. For "family" to be a useful metaphor for congregations in changing times, the term would need to be freed from our nostalgic longing for stable, homogeneous, and unchanging communities, with established structures and hierarchies of shared life. Luckily for us, the gospels suggest that Jesus invited people to cross boundaries, live into difference, and seek out brothers, and sisters, and mothers.

Watching people experiment with new ways of building networked faith communities raises a series of questions about our own congregations. Where does our information about the Christian life come from? Who can help us think in fresh ways about what congregations look like today and about what it means to follow Jesus into engagement with the needs of the world? Where do we engage theological and social difference? This raises questions about our local networks. Who are our neighbors? Are our switches open so that we can connect with and engage our neighbors? Are we receiving or blocking information about them, the challenges the community faces, and its resources to engage them? Does our congregation reflect the diversity of the community, and if not, why not?

A fluid networked culture provides ways for people to connect and shapes their expectations about relationships with people and institutions. This contributes to the tendency for people to be ecumenically and inter-religiously curious. They often network with more than one denomination or tradition. They may "follow" religious figures from other faiths and participate in worship outside their tradition. These networked connections, even if they are weaker, can be with more people and this exposes people to a greater diversity of belief and practice. The digital metaphor invites us to treat this religious diversity as a potential resource that can be sampled and integrated into our own faith identity and practice.

Good congregations are places where individuals feel known by and connect to God, find human relationships that sustain them, and purpose around a common story. People shaped by the fluid digital culture described above will have different expectations of what it means to participate with a congregation than did earlier generations. Yet, there continue to be people seeking the kind of connection and purpose congregations can offer. As your congregation reaches out to them, here are some things to expect.

A congregation may not be the only node in a person's spiritual network.

If your congregation seeks to serve fluid cultures, and attract people shaped by them, you have to be useful to people for whom the congregation will be but one part of their spiritual network. Those who seek out your congregation and participate with some regularity still may not join in with the same fervor and focus as traditional members. Many may see the life of the congregation, and the denominational tradition it represents, as one node in the network of sources they draw on in creating and performing their religious identity. They may visit other faith communities, follow religious blogs, or otherwise network with others. Think, for example, of some of the members of other congregations who follow *After Hours, Denver* and support their work with the homeless. For them, religious practice is not a zero-sum game in which only full dedication to a single node counts as faithful participation.

Rabbi David Teutsch describes the congregation as "one of many radiant centers."[14] Teutsch's phrase captures several important things about religious life in networked culture. First, the life of faith doesn't have a single institutional center. Secondly, these various networked centers must be radiant, that is they must connect us with something transcendent. His is a humble vision of community. The congregation doesn't have to meet everyone's need, for it is but one of many experiments. At the same time, it reminds us of the congregation's high calling. It must in some radiant way connect us to the Holy One.

They may come once, or sporadically.

Some people may be seeking an occasional engagement. They may "like" your congregation or pastor in a Facebook sense, that is by signaling approval and interest without necessarily desiring a closer relationship. For them, congregational life is one of many possible activities, competing with soccer or mountain biking. In their network, the congregation remains a fairly distant node. Think for instance of the "Christmas Eve and Easter" visitors who congregations and pastors often chide with the announcement that "we do this fifty-two weeks a year." The implication is that these worshipers are shallow, that their participation only has meaning if it leads them to regular attendance. What might happen if congregations welcomed their participation as a genuine spiritual expression, rather than treating them like consumers who should buy more of our religious product?

They may prefer short-term options.

Stable congregations tend to establish long term groups that often have vague end dates. People are invited to join Bible studies that have been meeting for years. If they agree to serve on a board or committee, it may be hard to get off. These are big asks of people seeking a more fluid relationship with the congregation. Having a rich mix of one-time volunteer opportunities and social events, short-term classes, and task forces that disappear when their project is completed provide more accessible entry points.

They will want to choose how to participate.

New people will not value some things that seem important to established folks. The traditional model of membership suggested an "all or nothing" commitment. Those who network with the congregation may be selective about which programs they attend and which preachers they come to hear. They may want to be connected without seeing membership as a necessary expression of their involvement. The congregation I attend has about 1,500 members, but one of our pastors says that "we think of ourselves as a church of 2,000." This suggests that fully a quarter of the people who are part of the congregation's network haven't chosen to join.

They may not follow our lead.

None of this suggests that people with these constructed religious identities, and who participate in congregations on their own terms, are not willing to serve and to lead. Networked congregations are open to the variety of ways people want to participate. They invite and welcome with less expectation about how people "ought" to respond. If membership and years of service are the price of having a voice in envisioning the future and of having opportunities to lead, we increase the likelihood that people will drift away to other more welcoming places in their network.

Resources are limited.

One challenge in a culture where people are less likely to center their lives of faith within a single religious institution is how we will support and sustain ministry. Even those deeply committed to existing forms of congregation cannot be driven only by the desire to sustain religious institutions. The call is to find faithful forms of Christian practice that make sense in contemporary culture. This likely requires that you find new ways of connecting with people and new ways of raising money. I will say a bit about that in the third section of this book.

If the church becomes a network of communications and relationships, what will that look like? Sometimes it will be short-term gatherings, as when my friend Michael died. A network of people in social media, most of whom I will never know, shared their stories and grief and in doing so they held me up during my own mourning and helped me celebrate my friend's life.

At other times, a network of relationships and the digital metaphor provide more lasting resources, as when they provided ways for the two brick-and-mortar congregations in Chicago to think about how their structures and habits impact their ability to welcome and engage their neighbors. Certainly, working on this requires new styles of leadership, and that is the focus of the next chapter.

DISCUSSION QUESTIONS

- In what places in your life do you experience the kind of deep and lasting relationships that typify traditional forms of community? Where do you experience more fluid networked relationships? What have these contributed to your life?
- In what ways are traditional assumptions about what religious community looks like embedded in your congregation's habits, programs, and expectations? Where have you established more fluid or networked practices? What are the implications of this?
- Do you see the need for your congregation to further adapt to networked culture? Why, or why not? What concrete changes would make your congregation more fluid, accessible, and welcoming?

5

Leadership and Authority

A small cookie and a land of milk and honey . . .

To make sense of what religious leadership looks like in a diverse and fluid digital culture, we will look at three interconnected things:

- Where are we going, that is, what vision guides us?
- Who leads us there, and what gives them the authority to do so?
- What form or style of leadership is useful in our context?

In the biblical account of the exodus, Moses led the early Hebrew people out of slavery in Egypt. Emboldened by direct encounters with God, who spoke to him from a burning bush and later on a mountaintop, he challenged the Pharaoh and laid out a vision of "a land of milk and honey." That vision motivated the people to follow him into unknown places to build a new social order. Still, Moses's authority is challenged and tested as the journey stretches out, and as it unfolds, he begins to share leadership with more people.

Like Moses, contemporary Christian leaders must help their people find a land they haven't seen and can only imperfectly imagine. The exodus from Egypt and the search for a promised land were frightening, and some early Hebrews wanted to return to Egypt (see Exodus 14:10–12). So it is today, some people want to return to the post–World War II successes of American congregations, the eighteenth century's Second Great Awakening, or some other idealized religious past. However, like Moses, visionary leaders help their community turn from nostalgia and look toward what they might become.

WHERE ARE WE GOING? WHAT VISION GUIDES US?

In chapters 3 and 4, we saw that tradition—particularly as a unified and guiding system—means less to people focused on constructing religious identity and building new forms of networked faith community than it does to those who find their identity within established communities. Yet even the innovators don't construct identity and community out of nothing. They try on faith practices, combine religious elements, and consider ideas drawn from religious traditions.

To a culture that primarily focuses on constructing new futures, religious traditions can seem like a museum of ancient curiosities, things that are interesting but no longer useful. However, looking at the religious identities and communities that people are building suggests that it is more accurate to think of tradition as a library of practices, material, and beliefs that might still point to God's presence.

Modern folks do relate to tradition, yet they do so in two distinctly different ways than people did in the past. First, people once saw tradition as a seamless inheritance that anchored them to a community; that is to say, they saw identity as a matter of who you identified with. In contrast, people formed by the digital metaphor think of identity as a unique construction; identity is seen as what sets them apart from other people. Second, earlier folks largely accepted the tradition as a package, whether as a Lutheran Christian or a Shia Muslim, they took on the tradition's worldview and practices. People today see the claims, material, and practices of a faith as things that can be accepted or rejected, and mixed and matched, with bits of other traditions.

Many modern practitioners think about the traditions they draw on as a storehouse of elements rather than as unified systems of thought and practice. But, for this library to be available, there must be people who maintain a vision of the tradition's coherence and beauty while—hopefully—critically engaging its limitations. These curators and teachers make the elements of the tradition available as resources that people can explore, experiment with, and incorporate into their religious identities.

Vision as Bodily Memory

How is a tradition passed on? Formal study is certainly one way that tradition is maintained, and its implications are understood. Learning about Christian history and your denomination or movement's discipline and practice tells us a lot. Yet a tradition is more than a set of faith claims, rules, and history to be learned in Sunday school or seminary. It is a constellation of shared mannerisms, tastes, moral intentions, and habits, what was called a *habitus* in chapter 4.

French novelist Marcel Proust gets at the way the senses evoke our past. In *In Search of Lost Time*,[1] he tells the story of how the taste of a *petite madeleine* (a small cookie) recalls his childhood sensations, brings back a flood of memories, and fills him with a sense of well-being. Religious tradition, as *habitus*, works similarly. Smells, tastes, sounds, or other sensations recall more than the claims of a faith system. They evoke the felt world of the tradition and call forth a bodily response. A friend, who had not been in worship in decades and does not describe herself as a believer, went to a beloved aunt's funeral mass. She reports that on entering the sanctuary, she was brought up short by the smell of candles lit for her aunt, the organ's sound, and the quality of light falling through stained glass. Without conscious intention, she genuflects and crosses herself as she slips into a pew. She says that in ways she didn't expect, but took solace from, she was—a least for a short time— drawn by sensual reminders and bodily memory back into her younger self's religious world.

Orthodox Christians are one group that grants particular authority to tradition. During a class visit to the Greek Orthodox cathedral described in chapter 1, Father Chris Margeritis was quick to distinguish Orthodox faith from Western Christianities by emphasizing that their theology and liturgy draws heavily on the early church fathers. Asked by a student about liturgical renewal, he asserts, "[O]ur liturgy is unchanged for 2,000 years. When it is perfect, why would you meddle?" For the Orthodox, and others who place a high value on tradition, religious identity is a matter of continuing ancient believers' practice. The repetition of the community's ancient creeds, the return to smells, images, and bodily habits evokes a sense of shared memory. These traditional practices shape the vision that guides them in changing times.

Other Christians give more attention to the effects of cultural change on religion. We have a stronger sense that the Christian tradition is multifaceted and has developed over time. If you accept that religion changes over time, it is a smaller step to assume that one can build a religious life by drawing on practices, materials, and concepts from multiple traditions. One example of a congregation that takes tradition quite seriously, while adapting it to a modern context, is *The House for all Sinners and Saints* (HFASS). This Denver congregation is rooted in a Lutheran expression of Christianity. They combine a hip blend of progressive urban identity and lifestyle, a desire for liturgy, and a commitment to shared leadership. Their website describes the way they put this together with an appreciation for tradition in this way:

We follow the ancient liturgy of the Church (chanting the Kyrie, reading from scripture, chanting the Psalm, sermon, prayers of the people, Eucharist, benediction, etc.). We also sing the old hymns of the Church. So, there's lots of ancient tradition at HFASS, but there's also some innovation. We always include poetry and a time called "Open Space" in which we slow down for prayer and other opportunities to actively engage the Gospel: writing in the community's Book of Thanks, writing prayers, making art, or assembling care kits for those experiencing homelessness.

You can learn more about HFASS's blend of tradition and innovation at http://houseforall.org/. Their curation of Lutheran theological method and liturgy is more than a matter of preserving past practices. They bring the resources of the tradition into conversation with the way society is changing. In doing so, HFASS creates a community where individuals, each on a faith journey, can imagine a shared future.

Vision as Speculation

There is value in understanding the habits and assumptions that have sustained generations and how the past can provide a vision for living today. It is also vital to picture where we are going. When Moses asked the ancient Hebrews to follow him out of Egypt, he told them that God would provide a place for them. However, he had not been to that "land of milk and honey" and had no map to show them where they would end up. Similarly, many people today believe that it is time to move on from habits and relationships that bind rather than liberate. And, like Moses, their leaders have to offer a compelling vision that will guide them on their journey.

I imagine frustrated readers demanding to know what vision the author proposes. In broad strokes, you can tease out how I imagine the church from what you have read. We are journeying toward a fluid and adaptive network. There, people and communities communicate something about how God is with us in the world through their messages, their embodied practices, and the on- and offline spaces and connections they construct. That network is a communion with earlier Christians and contemporaries who practice our faith in entirely different contexts. The church is also a network of conversations about how God is with us in our unique settings, our individual religious identity, and our shared practice. In the ebbs and flows of that networked communion and conversation, we find connections that bear us up and others that challenge our understanding and practice. I will say more about this in chapter 6.

Many of the experiments with both lasting and fleeting Christian communities discussed here seem to share some version of this broad vision.

However, the church as a network connects us with people motivated by different concepts of church. I don't imagine that this diverse conversation is building toward a single unified vision. It won't result in any sort of mega-denomination that could direct individuals and congregations. It is nuanced by the way people work out their relationships with tradition and context.

No leader has fully mapped the journey, or—to switch metaphors—has blueprints for the coming Christian community. We can't anticipate everything that is coming. Still, to lead through change, leaders must critique the current context—call out Pharaoh—and articulate a compelling future in which God accompanies us toward some land of milk and honey. While they have not resolved what the future will look like, visionary leaders and congregations experiment with options.

Those who seek to help congregations find a fresh vision learn things from their experience of digital culture and social networks. I discussed examples of this in the previous chapter. In the hope of more fluid congregations, they strive to lower the congregation's barriers so that it is easier for people to connect, they welcome those who may participate occasionally or only in a particular small group or program, they simplify and flatten the structures, and they give permission to those who want to try new things. Some innovators work on these things by building a more robust communications system, thinking both about the content and how to create an internal network that encourages multiple voices. Others seek to increase the congregation's network with its neighborhood or local community, make ecumenical and interfaith connections, and network with other Christian leaders and congregations who share their journey. All are needed.

For some leaders, these innovations don't go far enough or move quickly enough. They expect the death of congregations and denominations as we know them. They prefer to invest their energy in envisioning and experimenting with radical new online and face-to-face networks rather than in trying to fix the existing institutional church. It is useful for leaders and their followers to have honest conversations about whether they are seeking to perfect the congregation or envision other ways to form people's Christian self-understanding and shape their practice. I expect there to continue to be vital congregations even if their number shrinks. I also think that assuming that traditional, boundaried brick-and-mortar congregations are the only form of shared Christian life keeps us from seeing what else is emerging around us.

For example, chapter 1 opened with a discussion of *After Hours, Denver*, where people gather for theological conversation in bars and go out to feed the homeless in a city park. *After Hours*, is a vital experiment in Christian community and service that was launched with "new congregational start" money from the United Methodist Church. It is perhaps worth asking, does *After Hours* function as a congregation, as we have traditionally thought of congregations in the past? Is that what they are striving for? Or does that description create expectations *After Hours* can't meet and offer a distorted picture of their ministry? We might better understand projects like *After Hours* if we didn't expect them to grow into congregations; think of them instead as new interactive models of Christian connection and action. Doing so helps us better understand people's religious lives in the different circles that follow *After Hours*. How we think about *After Hours* and the various other pub theology and dinner church projects might expand the way we imagine Christian community and challenge our assumptions about what church can be in a culture of fluid connections.

Is the Institutional Church Part of the Vision?

Some of those who are thinking about the church's future, particularly those in the emerging church movement, are critical of what they call the *institutional church*. By institutional, they mean established congregations, whether independent or part of denominations (which are also part of the institutionalization of the church), the sort of congregation that typically meets in a designated sanctuary for weekly worship under the leadership of an ordained pastor. They distinguish the church as an institution, with its organizational structure, rules, and rigidities, from the church as a community of shared practice and belief. They often point to the house churches thought to be typical of the earliest Christians as an expression of the church's ideal form. They seek to build smaller, more flexible, and intimate forms of base Christian community.

There are real and understandable tensions between established churches and the people experimenting with new forms of a networked faith community. Denominations and congregations that hope to draw on these experiments' energy sometimes sponsor and support new ministry experiments—as was the case with *After Hours*. Their results are mixed. You hear the innovators' frustration in Steven Collins's discussion of the network the emerging church movement[2] was building early in the twenty-first century:

> There is no one leader or format or theology, nor is there likely to be. Instead, there is a thriving mess of cross-linkage without regard for conventional church structures or channels of communication. It's the context and lifeblood of the emerging church, . . . yet it's largely invisible to the existing institutional forms of church.

Collins cautions that what the innovators envision won't automatically be subsumed into existing congregations and denominations.

> This is what the institutional church fondly imagines will happen. It sees the emerging forms as parish churches in embryo. . . . Given time, encouragement, resourcing, they will grow the institution, even if it has to adapt to new appearances and behaviors.

He imagines there will be some networking with existing forms of church. However, for those creating new models of Christian connection and gathering, networking with denominations and traditional congregations is not necessarily the goal.

> This is what is happening. The emerging forms network across and around the institution. Some are connected into it, some are not and maybe don't want to be. Many of them will never be churches in the institutional understanding of the term, and attempts at making them so will damage or repel them. They are not so much churches as Church—Church as verb not noun.[3]

If Collins's vision of the church without institution is idealized, the frustration those involved have with expectations and structures that don't reflect their vision is real. When this happens, more traditional centers of ministry often lose these innovators and experimenters.

Today, the traditional congregation is but one of the multiple ways people envision a Christian community. Some people don't find congregations to be the most helpful place to work on their Christian self-understanding and shape their practice. They turn to different visions of community and formation. They may seek the structure and support of twelve-step groups, participate in short-term spiritual retreats or service projects, or develop online relationships with religious bloggers and their followers.

I expect there will continue to be vital brick-and-mortar congregations. However, assuming that they are the only or best form of shared Christian life can blind us to what else is emerging. Existing congregations cannot expect that those building new styles of Christian community will reach out to them. If congregations and their leaders want to be part of these alternative networks, they need to understand better the vision of what it means to "do church" that motivates experimenters and build conversations that include them.

For those of us who care about congregations, it is both liberating and frightening to recognize that there are other forms of Christian community. Our congregations are but some of the experiments with Christian community. It will be a significant challenge for traditional congregations and emerging Christian networks, whose visions of the church often differ significantly, to stay in conversation. It remains to be seen whether they believe they have anything to learn from each other. If they lose touch, the gap only widens.

WHO LEADS, AND WHAT GIVES THEM
THE AUTHORITY TO LEAD?

When authority is not equated so directly to a role or institutional authorization, or to traditional cultural markers like gender, age, or race, there is more room for new leaders. These new leaders are followed by people who recognize and admire their charisma, vision, and skill set. This shift in leadership challenges existing hierarchies. Lay folks who trust their own perceptions are less likely to wait for clergy to set the vision. They often move forward to reshape their congregations and denominations. Through their personal networks and connections, they build alternative religious spaces outside congregational or denominational structures.

About a decade ago, I was involved in a research project that interviewed Muslim and Christian community leaders in the Mountain West. We asked the Muslims how they were developing uniquely American and modern forms of Islamic identity and practice.[4] The Muslims were respectful of the role of the *imam* within the mosque. Still, they did not expect that these mostly foreign-born and traditionally educated clerics would guide their community into practices that made sense in the modern digital American culture they inhabited. They assumed that conversations about what it meant to be Muslim and American would happen primarily outside the mosque. They followed rising on- and offline voices that explored what modern Muslims' lives might look like. This process narrows the imam's role, creates new Islamic spaces, reduces the community's focus on past practice, and assumes cultural adaptation and change. We found that Christian leaders were often less aware than their Muslim neighbors that they inhabit a new and different culture. Still, their need to adapt to digital culture produces a similar pattern in which those who understand the emerging culture create spaces to talk about what it means to practice one's religious identity within one's roles in the family and society.

"Mom bloggers," are another example of this democratization of leadership. Often writing about their religious identity and practice but functioning outside the boundaries of congregation or denomination, they offer confessional and advice-giving reflections on their own experience as stay-at-home or working parents. They are not ordained, nor do they hold degrees in child development, but millions of women follow them. With online advertising and the sale of books or other products, mom blogging has become a lucrative career for some.

One example of a highly successful mom blogger with a progressive Christian perspective is Glennon Doyle. Doyle, then Glennon Doyle Melton, began blogging under the witty title *Momastery*[5] in 2009. Her confessional reflections on her experience as a parent and spouse, and on her divorce and subsequent marriage to U.S. Soccer star Abby Wambach, became the core of an online conversation that grew into what Doyle describes as "the Momastery community." Parenting and relationship are, in these reflections, often tricky and messy. Doyle doesn't present herself as perfect, or even as an expert. She is a fellow traveler with other women embedded in family systems and inspired and supported by a loving and grace-filled God. Today she connects with the Momastery blog community through the *Huffington Post*, three books—one an Oprah pick—and personal appearances.

Doyle has become a larger public figure than most mom bloggers, but observing the phenomenon lets us see how command of new media gives people with a provocative perspective and voice religious authority and social presence. When those who blog from a faith perspective—whether it is a progressive Christian mom like Doyle, or an evangelical, Muslim, or Jewish mom—find a following, they gain a kind of authority within their faith communities and sometimes in the wider society. Many of these women are also involved in congregations, but the mom blogs and the conversations they generate create an alternative space where women have a voice and can imagine together what it means to practice faith in daily life. In doing so, they blur the line between professional ministry and lay leadership.

Considering the mom bloggers and Muslim community leaders and their influence can help us think about religious life in digital culture. First, they model the way community grows around shared experience, here the experience of immigrants working out hyphenated identities as Muslim Americans and women whose religious identity is shaped by their experiences as partners and mothers. Second, we see that authority is not granted based on credentials but in response to an authentic and creative reflection that affirms the community's experience and helps them find their way in the world. Third, whether involved in traditional faith communities or not, charismatic leaders create alternative spaces for conversation and community. When we ask who helps form people's religious identity, practice, and communities, we can't just think about traditional forms of religious leadership.

In the emerging models, many people participate in developing and articulating a vision of the congregation's life. When people are open to their diverse gifts or charisma, there can be multiple parish leaders. Some will rise to momentary situations, others will organize ongoing congregational practices, and some will articulate a vision and motivate the community to sustained work. For a small example, I know of a congregation where two laywomen saw a need for silent meditation. They organized a modest group experience that meets each Wednesday evening in an otherwise little-used chapel. The group is not large, but the participants value it. Now the congregation's midweek programming is planned around this gathering. The clergy have had the good sense not to take it over, or manage it, but to recognize the lay leadership that brought it into being. As we have seen, if congregations don't welcome their leadership, they are likely to move on to create alternative religious spaces.

Clergy

When someone says, "[D]o what I say, because I am your parent," or "boss," or "pastor," they are asserting role authority. It is what people in the military mean when they say that "you salute the uniform." In the past, respect for their title and role granted clergy a good deal of hierarchal authority to direct the life of congregations and denominations and as moral arbitrators. That respect and authority came at a cost; clergy were often "put on a pedestal" by their followers. They dressed and presented themselves in prescribed ways, kept a certain distance, and maintained a firm distinction between the personal and the professional. Thus, when I entered a seminary in the mid-1970s, one of my pastors offered to buy me a black suit, and in class, faculty cautioned us against making friends within the congregation.

In many ways today, clergy have come down or been taken down from the pedestal. The distinctions between the pastor and congregants that the black suit and caution about friendships were meant to maintain begin to break down. Role authority must be confirmed relationally. Whether the leader is compelling, engaging, and trustworthy is more important that traditional credentials. It is more helpful for pastors to use persuasive power rooted in their relationships, gifts, character, and track record. Like other leaders, clergy adopt more informal relational styles, and they are less able to make, or less interested in making, firm distinctions between the personal and the professional.

The changes described above better match our culture, I think they are largely positive and generally inevitable. Yet, in some ways the shift in relational style complicates the role of pastors and other professional religious leaders. Pastoral theologian David Hogue comments, "I find myself continuing to be wary of pastoral friendships in the community—less from an authority and distancing perspective and more from a family systems bias that recognizes the diffuse ways in which power is constructed and implemented in those complicated relationships."[6]

One result of bringing clergy down from their pedestal is pastors' readiness to describe their struggles with confessional honesty. Rather than presenting a completely idealized self, they demonstrate how insight arises in their journey of faith. We see this approach among online opinion leaders, and it is increasingly evident in the pulpit. Some pastors confess their histories with addictions, and many make their struggle with faith questions part of their modeling of an authentic and integrated Christian life. Thus, they signal that Christianity is not an all-or-nothing package, but rather an ongoing series of choices and actions through which identity is clarified and performed. Done well, this invites followers into a conversation about their own religious identity and practice and how their daily living shapes their belief.

Of course, other factors than media change also shape our expectations of leaders. For instance, there are increasing numbers of women among the clergy. Some combination of resistance to their leadership and embrace of the way feminists and womanists have thought about leadership shapes contemporary religious life. Today, clergy authority rests more on people's recognition that the leader is a trustworthy guide, is personally engaging, and lives and leads out of a compelling vision of how God is at work in people and the world. If designated leaders don't display these characteristics, people are unlikely to follow them because they hold a theological degree, an ordination certificate, or a title. Clergy people continue to have authority, but they receive it and express it differently from early generations.

Today clergy can seldom dictate what individuals and the congregations should do, yet this does not mean they are without significant power. They are positioned to articulate a vision of what the church can be and invite individuals and communities to join them in faithful discernment practices as they seek to envision and embody God's people at work in contemporary culture. Leaders who were acculturated to old hierarchical and role-related styles of leadership sometimes have difficulty developing this conversational form of leadership. Accepting that they cannot dictate, they come to see themselves only as managers of institutions and conversations. Yet, we see that strong leaders must be able to speak with a clear voice, to challenge certain practices and decisions, and at times to speak on behalf of the tradition.

Understanding Authority Today

The word "authority" has the same old French root as "author."[7] We might say that individuals who are constructing religious identity take the authority to author themselves. People also give authority to those they follow. To be an authority is to produce something, be the author of something, in the individual follower, and the community's life.

The gospels tell us that Jesus "taught them as one having authority" (Matthew 7:29 NRSV, also Mark 1:22). The literature on preaching and church leadership is full of reflections on the source and nature of that authority and speculation on what this tells us about how today's leaders should lead. Some people see Jesus's power as a matter of his human appeal and charisma. Others claim that in him the scriptures are fulfilled. This understanding roots his authority in that of the Jewish tradition and its sacred texts. Still others argue that Jesus's authority is a product of his divinity, that through Jesus, people heard the word of God. However one understands this, it is worth noting that Jesus did not hold an official role in the synagogue or society. His was not the sort of authority imposed by law or role. People who followed Jesus found him to be a useful teacher and leader. It could be said that, not unlike online followers, Jesus's followers granted him authority.

Who has the authority to lead Christian communities today? Much of the literature on leadership treats it as a professional skill. Thus, people sometimes frame discussions of religious leadership as being about the role of the clergy or others paid to maintain the institutional church's life. However, when we look at the range of religious leaders today, ordained clergy and other trained religious professionals are far from the only ones involved in forming the Christian life. People without formal credentials, ordination, or education, who are motivated by a vision of what church might become, are taking authority to lead. We see this clearly within emerging religious networks but also within existing congregations. Digital culture's emphasis on charisma and voice encourages this shift away from role authority and blurs the distinction between professional and volunteer vocational leaders.

In fact, in the construction of the religious self, and deciding whether and how they participate in congregations and other groups, it is clear each person is her or his own leader. They claim the authority to integrate or reject beliefs and practices and set a personal spiritual trajectory. At the same time, they network with each other, connecting and "following" those to whom they grant authority.

Accountability

People want trustworthy leaders that help them discern God's leading and develop faithful practice. The focus on individual autonomy produces charismatic leaders with a high sense of personal authority. In religious communities this charisma is often seen as the evidence of a unique connection to God. Charismatic leaders, who are not anchored by some system of institutional or communal accountability, trust in their personal integrity and sense of what feels right. However, self-interest often blinds people to the good. Today we are deeply aware that power can distort vision and be abused. Clergy financial and sexual scandals have left a legacy of distrust.

The question of building trustworthy systems of accountability is further complicated when we think of the way leadership and voice are shared in networked systems. It is no longer a matter of holding a few key leaders who hold power accountable—important as that is! Now faith communities, whether structured as traditional congregations or online gatherings, must think about how to support and hold accountable a range of people who lead in a variety of ways.

Trustworthiness is not merely a matter of character. The reliability of individual leaders and particular institutions rests on systems of transparency and accountability. It is here that, for all their failings, established institutions and denominations have an advantage. They typically have clear policies and expectations and have systems of accountability with the power to punish transgressors. Indeed, these have sometimes erred on the side of protecting those in power from shame and loss of authority. But increasingly, the voices of victims are heard, and established communities are clarifying systems of accountability. When institutions of accountability break down, we lose the systems that can call us to account for transgressions.

One purpose of a community is to create a web of accountability. It behooves us to think about how a loosely networked Christianity can do that. It is much harder for emerging independent congregations and communities, particularly those built around charismatic leaders, to establish robust systems of accountability. We saw this demonstrated during the rise of evangelical television broadcasting. When charismatic leaders crossed boundaries, there were no accountability systems to constrain their excesses and violations: the distance, diffusion, and lack of sustained community in digital culture further compound these issues.

Online shaming of boundary-crossing leaders may be digital culture's effort to create some sort of accountability. Surely, we can do better! Those building new forms of Christian community today need to depend on more than a leader's personal character. This won't be easy. It requires clear conversations that lead to establishing accountability systems in networks that value their independence and lack of institutional structure. Yet it is imperative. This work requires leaders' self-awareness and reflection and developing clarity of expectation within individual communities and in the networks that unite them.

WHAT FORM OR STYLE OF LEADERSHIP
DOES OUR CONTEXT CALL FOR?

Each leader probably has a personal style of leadership within which they are most comfortable. However, just as the rise of digital culture made some ways of thinking of personal identity and community seem natural and others hard to sustain, this fluid culture encourages a leadership style that at least appears to be democratic.

What Social Media Teaches

As is evident in the discussion above, the rise of social media and the emergence of the digital metaphor have challenged common assumptions about who has voice and influence. Media savvy clergy learn things from their own experience of digital culture and from observing the often uncredentialled leaders who emerge there. Digital culture encourages a quite different leadership style, public presence, and personal/professional boundaries than they were taught in seminary or saw modeled by earlier generations of clergy. Many clergy folks seek—or are pushed by people in their congregations—to adopt more democratic styles of shared leadership. They resist the idea that their role lets the clergy decide for the congregation. Instead, they function as resources to the faith community. They see their theological education and Christian formation as preparation to be curators of traditions and coaches of individuals and communities. They draw on inherited and emerging ideas to inspire and offer possibilities for practice and interpretation. Together with those with whom they serve, they envision a faithful future.

Helping established congregations adapt to a new, more networked style is not easy. Pastors and lay leaders are human. They have self-interest and don't easily give up power. Some current members will be uncomfortable with a less formal style and resist sharing more fully in making congregational decisions. Anxiety about change and the congregation's viability encourages the sense that we need a strong leader; if things are not improving, we have the wrong leader.

Clergy who seek to have a broader presence in networked society also create blogs, Twitter accounts, podcasts, and Facebook pages that reach beyond their congregations. By combining online and offline presence and adopting a leadership style that invites discussion, they create alternative channels of relationship that connect them to people both inside and outside the boundaries of their congregations. Together leaders, individuals, and communities envision Christian practice in a culture shaped by its experience of interactive digital communications.

For example, two former Iliff School of Theology students blog as "The Bearded Theologians." Zach Bechtold is a pastor in Wyoming and Matt Franks is the pastor of a community in Oklahoma. As "The Beards," they have developed a voice outside their parishes and a broader influence on other pastors and lay followers. You can learn about them, click on a podcast, or purchase a Bearded Theologian beer mug or T-shirt at beardedtheologians .com/.

LEADERSHIP AS CEASELESS SPEAKING

Some see the democratization of religious leadership as a turn away from traditional models of Christian leadership. However, it may be that the earliest Christian communities provide models for our contemporary networked society. The theologian, poet, and former Archbishop of Canterbury Rowan Williams says that in early Christianity, authority was located in what he calls the churches' "obsessive" networks of communication. He describes a unity forged by a steady flow of communication, a connection established in letters that argued genuine theological and experiential differences.[8] Like the earliest Christians, people in today's networked digital culture live in a time when a way forward is being found through a network of discussion and debate. If the church is, and has been, a network of communities ceaselessly speaking with each other, leaders must strive to generate, curate, and keep this conversation open. I will turn to Williams's provocative suggestion in the next chapter where I briefly explore what a theology for a networked church might look like.

DISCUSSION QUESTIONS

- The author suggests that in less-hierarchical systems, "everyone has authority over their construction of the religious self, and over whether and how they participate in congregations. . . . Each is, in this sense, his or her own leader." Is this the case for you and for people you know?
- In your congregation and broader circles, is leadership primarily about charisma, about following appealing voices, and not about systems that train and ordain or certify leaders? What are the advantages and disadvantages of these ways of identifying leaders?
- Who has authority to lead in your congregation and where does it come from? What is the role of clergy, laypersons who hold official positions, and informal leaders? How are these negotiated?

- Today, in the age of "Me Too," we are aware that faith communities have the same issues as other institutions with abuses of power. What are your expectations of faith leaders? What makes a leader trustworthy? How, and to whom, are leaders accountable in your faith community? What unique challenges are faced by the independent communities that gather around charismatic figures?

III

REIMAGINING THE CONGREGATION

6

A Brief Theology of the Church as Network

The churches' ceaseless speaking to, with, and for one another . . .

Three key ideas shape this chapter:

- The Holy Spirit, as the active presence of God in the world, is discovered in the conversation of faith communities trying to engage God in their unique contexts.
- The church, as it listens to the promptings of the Spirit, is an incubator of Christian practices of worship, care, service, and justice.
- The church has been, from its beginning, a fluid network of conversation about practice.

Earlier chapters describe some implications of digital culture and make a pragmatic case for developing Christian practices that make sense to people shaped by our contemporary media context. They reflect on the contemporary focus on personal religious identity that is often constructed from elements taken from multiple sources, the looser and more fluid forms of community that are typical of digital culture, and the new models of religious leadership that are emerging within that culture. Understandably, these shifts in how people practice their faith may have left some readers wondering whether these sometimes-diffuse forms of networked religious life remain Christian in any recognizable form. You may well ask, what understanding of Christian life and connection holds these discussions of religious identity, community, and leadership together?

In response, this chapter lays out a brief theology of the church as network. This understanding of the church rests on the assumption that the Holy Spirit is always doing a new thing and that the work of the Spirit links us to new people and situations in order that those who follow Jesus might continue to bear witness to love and justice in a changing world. Understood in this way, the church—attentive to this work of the Spirit—serves as an incubator of Christian practices of care, service, and justice making. This cultivation of Christian practice happens within a shifting and expanding network of conversation about what the faith looks like in particular contexts. Thus, in real and observable ways, Christian practice has changed and will continue to change where the Spirit interacts with specific cultures. These changes lead to new understandings of God's activity in the world. What remains unchanging is God's invitation to live into new possibilities. Looking back on tradition from the vantage point of the contemporary struggle to be faithful in our context reveals both continuities and contrasts with what the church has looked like in the past. Engaging and exploring what we hold in common with those who went before us, and taking seriously how our contexts are different, puts the work of the Spirit in cultural context. This can provide fresh understandings of the gospel, the nature of the early church, and of the experience of people in different times and places than our own, that illuminate our own struggle to perceive what God is doing among us.

Because an understanding of the Holy Spirit is essential to understanding the church amid change, it is necessary to say a bit more about what I mean by the term. The Spirit is the way God is actively present in the world today and in history. In the gospel accounts, Jesus speaks of the Spirit when before his death/resurrection/ascension he tells the disciples, "I will send a comforter" or in some translations "an advocate" (John 14:16). My thinking about this is influenced by the work of my former doctoral student Jeremy Garber. He is a Mennonite, part of the larger Anabaptist tradition that shares a very high sense of the importance of community. Garber claims that the Holy Spirit can be understood as "the communal creation and transmission of meaning in a Christian minoritarian context." Further, he says, "The Spirit is not only the *result* of God's action in the world, but also the cause of action in that world. The Holy Spirit is the . . . source of inspiration and power." How do we know when it is the Spirit that inspires? Garber says that the Holy Spirit bears "definitive signs of love, peace, justice, and joy."[1] He is arguing, and I largely agree, that this active work of God in the world that we call the Holy Spirit is only—or at least most fully—found in the conversation of faith communities trying to engage God in their unique contexts. You can see how useful this is to my sense of Christianity as a networked way of life rather than primarily a matter of doctrines of belief.

LIQUID CHURCH

Chapter 4 drew on Pete Ward's distinction between a solid institutional church and the liquid church that innovators imagine and are beginning to create in digital cultures. Ward argues that the solid church, characterized by buildings, denominations, and institutional structure, is increasingly a museum to a dying way of Christian life. In its place, Ward foresees a liquid church that exists online and in occasional gatherings and borrowed spaces, one with minimal formal structure and maximal innovation, connection, and movement. It is, he suggests, fluid and thus able to flow into new on- and offline spaces, thus adapting to the contours of emerging digital cultures.

There is, in Ward's vision, both a critique of the failings of the institutional church and a celebration of the more fluid possibilities of digital culture. Both should be taken seriously.

Ward suggests that Christians who are attentive to their location in cultures shaped by the digital are journeying toward a fluid and adaptive network of faith, one where people and communities communicate about how God is with us in the world through their messages and their embodied practices in the on- and offline spaces and connections they construct. This seems to propose a radical new understanding of the body of Christ. However, perhaps this is not entirely new. The social media networks where this communicating and connecting is happening may illustrate an ancient understanding that Christian theology has long claimed, that for the church to be its true self it must continually be defined by what God is doing in the world around us. Because of this, the church "universal" that connects us to Christians of other times and places, is also local, that is, it is shaped by what God calls forth in particular times and contexts.

Theologian Serene Jones speaks to this when she says the church is

> undone by the word of God that breaks in upon it. This community, therefore, does not possess itself but always receives itself from God. This community doesn't own the terms by which it is collected, named, and defined; these too it receives. This community's core identity cannot therefore be defined by kinship ties, geographic region, and ethnicity. . . . Thus, at a fundamental level, this church knows itself to be constituted by its intrinsic openness to God.[2]

The church can never be understood solely as my local church, denomination, or even all those who practice the faith today, As Jones says, these draw us to define the church by kinship, location, and ethnicity. The church is, to use a metaphor from digital culture, always a wider network that draws our local experience of the God at work into conversation with what God is doing in other places and times. It cannot be adequately understood by our memory of its past practice and of what God once did. These inheritances from the past are interpreted and critiqued by what God is doing today. The church, understood as the body of Christ, is a wider communion that connects us with earlier Christians and with contemporaries who practice the faith in entirely different contexts, and which foresees a connection with those who will come after us and practice the faith in ways not yet imagined. This networked church is fluid because God is active. The body of Christ is an ongoing conversation about what God is doing among us. In the ebbs and flows of these larger and local networked communions and conversations, Christians find connections that both bear us up and challenge our understanding and practice.

THE CHURCH AS NETWORK OF COMMUNICATION

It may be that the fluid and networked church that we are beginning to experience helps us to see the earlier Christian communities more clearly. In fact, there are continuities between their practice and that of people of faith in our contemporary networked society. Theologian, poet, and former Archbishop of Canterbury Rowan Williams says that in early Christianity, authority was not located in Rome or Jerusalem, that is, not in the voice of a single authoritative figure, but in what he calls the churches' "obsessive" networks of communication. He describes a unity forged by a steady flow of communication, a connection established in letters that articulated genuine theological and experiential differences. Williams suggests that "authority is made in the churches' ceaseless speaking to, with, and for one another."[3] Spiritual director Diane Stephens Hogue responds to Williams's suggestion with the reminder that the process also requires listening, both to each other and for the voice of God. This process of speaking and listening roots the church in fluid possibilities and draws our attention to how new practices and ways of relating reveal fresh understandings of the movement of the Spirit among us. It also may suggest the churches' long desire to solidify, to build institutions, and finalize credal statements comes at a cost, that it masks the Spirit's fluid movement.

Williams's provocative claim is that the nature of the church is most fully revealed in its ongoing conversation rather than in the conclusions of a key leader or church council. In this way of thinking, the church is not an accomplishment, some project that was or will ever be finished, but rather a process. As did those early followers of Jesus, people in today's networked digital culture live in a time when a way forward is being found through what seems like "ceaseless speaking." In conversation with the traditions of practice and belief that we have inherited, our contemporary context, and the future that is yet being revealed, God's people speak, and experiment, and speak some more about what the Holy One is doing among us.

What does this ceaseless conversation look like, how does it respond to the needs of the times, and what are its implications? I found myself thinking about this as I watched the PBS program *The Black Church: This Is Our Story, This Is Our Song.*[4] Over two 2-hour episodes, host, historian, and literary critic Henry Louis Gates Jr. teases out the development of Black Christianity in the United States. He does not use the language of network or draw on theories of mediation to describe how the church is maintained and extend through speaking, song, and bodily practice. Yet, Gates paints a picture of the church, at least as it exists in Black communities, as a network of connection and resistance to racism and white supremacy that changes and adapts as it hears the word of God in the changing contexts of Black people in America. Gates reminds us that when Africans were enslaved and brought to the Americas, they were not a single people with a common language or religion. Gates suggests that development of Black Christianity provides the network through which they begin to connect and through which they hear God's judgment on their enslavement. They take up the religious symbols and stories of their oppressors, bring them into conversation with their own heritage and condition, and find the God who led enslaved people out of Egypt doing a very different thing than their white oppressors anticipate. To overly simplify a complex story, a developing Black Christianity existed as a network of practice and gathering during slavery. From that network congregations and denominations later develop and serve as links in a web that holds the community together through emancipation, Jim Crow, and later the Great Migration. Gates demonstrates that this network of ethical and theological conversation, which produces the Black Church, both preserves a tradition of interpretation and adapts to cultural change as the fluid network of Black Christianity listens for the voice of God in new contexts.

The Civil Rights Movement is an example of how in the face of oppression networked communities connect, communicate, and act. This web linked people across denominational lines and drew white allies into the movement. The network is not a respecter of religious boundaries; Gates demonstrates how the movement created conversations and enabled shared action with Jews and Black Muslims. More recently, with the Black Lives Matter movement, Gates notes that it is not so clear that the Black church still leads the community's struggle for racial justice. Yet, it remains a voice in a wider network of struggle in a changing community.

FUTURE CHURCH

Of course, we are anxious to see where this web of speaking will take us. We want to discover whether these fluid connections and conversations will have sustaining and formative power in our lives. We want to know what sort of caring communities they are producing and whether they have enough substance to sustain us and unite us in the church's work for justice and peace. These are important questions, and people should rightly measure the new forms of Christian life by the fruits they bear. Yet, to give ourselves to a networked community maintained by "ceaseless speaking" is to be committed to process. Like the early followers of Jesus, like Black Christians who challenge systems of oppression and adapt to change, all Christians must attend to what God is doing among us while not fully understanding where the journey will take us. Rowan Williams's description of the early Christians describes the church, from its beginning, as a community that is revealed in and defined by its experimentation and conversation. At any moment, we must be rigorous in describing what it is with all its possibilities and limits, and we must discern what it is becoming, and be open to correction and change.

If the church is characterized by its ceaseless speaking, what is it that Christians are ceaselessly speaking about? We tell stories of God's past faithfulness and discuss the application of these stories today. Further, the conversation is on what God is currently doing in people's individual lives and communities and about what God will yet do in us and through us in the future. In America, what God is doing is inseparable from the legacy of slavery, Jim Crow, civil rights struggles, and the insistence that Black lives matter. Widening our network, and softening our boundaries, can create space for white Christians to think about how the Spirit is moving and about what forms of Christian practice link, or block, us from being attentive to that movement of the Spirit.

What God has done and is bringing about is a web of relationships. Matthew's gospel imagined it as the kingdom of heaven, other biblical language thinks of it as a family in which we are sisters and brothers and neighbors. This suggests that the clearest picture of what God is doing and will do is revealed in relationships. We see this most easily in our ties to family and geographic neighbors, yet this vision of the church suggests that we are also in networked conversations with those who practiced our faith in previous generations and with contemporary communities and cultures far different from our own. And because the God who is involved in the world today, judging its failings and loving it into new possibilities, will continue to do new things in the future, we are networked, at least implicitly, with those who come after us and with what they and God will do in contexts we do not yet imagine.

There is a critique of congregations as we have known them in the model of a fluid and wide-ranging church. Congregations are inherently local and often defined by kinship ties, ethnicity, and region in ways that limit their vision of the fullness of the relational network of God. Yet the relational God who is engaged with people in their unique cultural and historical contexts calls them into wider networks of connection.

The concept that the universal church has a broader vision of what God is doing among us than do individual localized congregations must also be critiqued. The "universal church" is an ideal vision that has never yet been accomplished. Further, much of what we know about how algorithms drive people toward like-minded folks raises questions about whether and to what degree virtual religious communities are more diverse than face-to-face institutional faith communities. Do online networked faith communities better reproduce the fluid faith community of conversation about God and human religious practice that Ward, Jones, and Williams describe? It is an open question. Some will argue that the narcissistic focus on the individual, the shallowness and nastiness of many online interactions, and the secularity of the times argue against this. It would be naïve not to take these challenges seriously. Yet in digital culture there is also the promise of network, of new ways of relating that provide the opportunity to find and connect with other experimenters.

Clearly, some individuals and congregations simply resist or reject this image of a fluid and networked church that focuses on what God is doing among us today, embraces change, and is empowered by a vision of a still-unfolding future that we see only "through a glass darkly" (I Corinthians 13:12 KJV). They give more attention and authority to the powerful accounts of what God has done in the past and to clearer boundaries of identity and inclusion. Those who do find this vision of a networked and fluid community of faith compelling and who believe that it helps them make sense of contemporary digital cultures seem to proceed in two ways. Some remain hopeful that traditional congregations and perhaps even traditional denominations can adapt their theology and practice in ways that will make them vital elements in the network of faith. While networking beyond the local church, they continue to invest in helping congregations adapt. Others are skeptical that this can happen or that it is worth the effort. They may wish those working in congregations well, but they put their own efforts into building new and more fluid, often virtual, relationships.

There are practical reasons for this split between those who remain committed to ongoing work within existing congregations and those who envision and strive for new forms of Christian connection and practice. Everyone's time, theological imagination, and other resources are limited, and people must make choices about where to invest. However, what we know about the "both/andness," of how people adapt to the possibilities of virtual connection in general suggests that there is no underlying reason to think that the church can be solely defined either by its network or the congregations that are nodes of its web. People who Zoom with Grandma don't stop wanting to visit when they can. The fact that some kinds of work can be done online does not mean there are not times when it is better to meet in embodied face-to-face gatherings. It seems likely that for the foreseeable future, much of the church's "ceaseless speaking to, with, and for one another" will be about these various ways of connecting and on the practices they teach and their effect on their communities.

An Implicit Theology of Practice

One implication of envisioning the church as a forward-focused debating society or laboratory of innovation is that Christian practices proceed and teach Christian identity and belief. Rather than thinking that one must first be formed by learning doctrine and then proceed to act out of shared beliefs, the church as network draws people into Christian practice and then has conversation about the implications of these practices for their and the community's identity. We perhaps understand this best through observation. At saint benedict's table (https://stbenedictstable.ca/), an Anglican parish in Winnipeg who prefer their name uncapitalized, the communion table is open to all. This contravenes the Anglican teaching that the eucharist should be offered only to those who are baptized and confirmed in their faith. Asked about this, Rector David Widdicombe recalls the congregation's first gathering. There were nine people present including two children, one baptized and one unbaptized. He recalls, "We'd said we were going to gather around the eucharistic table" and remembers asking himself, "Am I *not* going to incorporate this child?" The rector speaks of saint ben's experience in a very networked way. It is, he says, one "of being drawn to the table and having that fellowship extend to other tables" and that "[w]e always meet over meals. . . . It changes things."[5] The implicit theology that seems to guide saint ben's is a trust that this unbaptized child will be formed by coming with the community to the table and sharing in what is offered there, that this will lead the child to other ways of serving, and to an embodied understanding of him- or herself as a follower of Jesus with faith in the God met at the table. I do not argue that this is the only right way to think about the sacrament, nor that it is a new understanding, or that Widdicombe came to it from some overt reflection on digital culture. Yet, it is illustrative of the logic inherent in so much of digital culture.

In the church as network, formation happens in a combination of talking about doubt, belief, and identity, *and* in trying out practices. We also saw this in the earlier discussion of *After Hours, Denver*'s pub gatherings and ministry to the homeless. Whether it is a pub theology group, an online blog, a conventional Sunday School class, the chance to be a shepherd in the Christmas pageant, or to work on a Habitat for Humanity house, faith communities are providing spaces for people to imagine and perform Christian identity. This is not new; what is distinctive is the way folks in networked culture understand what they are striving for. Though we are all shaped by the communities we network with, the focus of people shaped by contemporary digital culture stays on the individual. They may affiliate with congregations, even join them, but they are not likely to see the congregation or tradition as a whole package of belief and practice to be adopted.

The Virtual Body of Christ

People bring their doubts, questions, and explorations into the community. When they are met there by compassionate people who share their own struggles and resources, the congregation becomes a source to be mined and a conversation partner. These conversations require humility and honesty from those who preach and teach. A congregation where this happens can be thought of as a network of individuals who value their connection. At the same time a wider view sees that the people within such congregations also network with other sources and conversation partners. The congregation is most effective at drawing people in and building relationships when they understand their role as supporting people in their own ongoing process of forming and practicing Christian identity.

Deanna A. Thompson says that she was skeptical of the claim that meaningful Christian communities could exist and be maintained in online spaces. In part this is because she has a high and focused expectation of the church. If the church matters, it must be making a difference in the lives of those who suffer. How, she wondered, "can we build a culture of trust, support, and healing around the broken and hurting in our midst," in spaces that she thought of as imaginary or unreal? In *The Virtual Body of Christ in a Suffering World*[6] she describes how reflection on an extended period of profound illness led her to argue against the distinction between the "virtual" church and the "real" or "actual" church. In pain, bedridden, and contemplating her own mortality, she was radically dependent on others for care and support. Reflecting on this experience, she writes, "It was shocking to realize that through virtual connectedness via a website I was surrounded by a cloud of witnesses greater than any I could have imagined."[7] Reflection on how the church was present in people who were physically present, bringing food for her family, sitting with her to visit and pray *and* in people who followed her illness online, praying from a distance, and perhaps texting or writing letters expanded her sense of the incarnation and of what it means to live incarnationally. There is, she says, no clear divide between offline and online realities.

Thompson cites Jason Byassee's reflection on Paul's letter to the Corinthians[8] to argue that the incarnational presence of Christ has always meant more than physical proximity. Paul, far away and unable to be physically present, longed to be with the church he founded in Corinth. Byassee notes that Paul does not wait until he could travel to them; rather, he wrote compelling letters, reminding them of their connection and calling them to a better practice of their faith. Those messages, which Rowan Williams describes as part of the church's ceaseless speaking to one another, are part of the network of relationship of caring and communication that binds the Corinthians to Paul and us to these early followers of Jesus.

Can the church exist in a network of shifting online relationships? Thompson answers that since the time of Paul, the body of Christ has always been a virtual body. Though its members were not always physically present to one another, they were nevertheless part of the same catholic community. She acknowledges that because virtual presence today often comes through digital technology, many Christian leaders warn of the dangers of disembodied existence. Arguing theologically from her own experience and observation she challenges the claim that virtual presence via digital technology is necessarily an inferior form of presence.

THE CONCRETE CHURCH

If the body of Christ is virtual, or at least can be virtual, and if the best theological understandings of the church sees it as a fluid network, what are we to make of the very concrete congregations and denominations that own buildings, have bylaws and hierarchies and boundaries? Are such congregations still the right location for the "communal creation and transmission of meaning" that Garber says is the presence of the Holy Spirit among us? It is easy to get the relationship between the concrete and the spiritual wrong. In the next chapter I will argue with those innovators who, frustrated by the institutional church's rigidities, imagine that they are easily separated and that it is possible to build a purely virtual and spiritual communion. It is also necessary to critique those who so unite the spiritual and the concrete that they resist change by treating the human-created structures of the church as divinely imposed rigidities. People of color, women, and gay and lesbian folk rightly remind us that the church has a long history of resisting the Holy Spirit's reforming work.

Seeking to balance the value of form and of the fluid network I have been describing, practical theologian David Hogue asked me if the network is durable enough to sustain the church without some structure.[9] It is an appropriate and helpful question. Formal congregations, with their structures of worship, formation, fellowship, and service, have played an important role in my life and in the lives of many. I have also known congregations that were staid, wedded to the past, and resistant to what God seemed to be doing in their wider communities. Though I do not think they will all survive in our more secular age, nor that they are the only form of Christian community, they remain an important part of the web of practice and belief that forms and connects Christians. For those embedded in congregations, the challenge is to understand what it is about their structure and form that blinds them to the Spirit's work among us and to reform them so that they are freed to respond and adapt to cultural change and God's response. Those seeking to build new forms of on- and off-line Christian community should understand that their new ways of relating may be less structured, but they also require form and leadership. As have been congregations and denominations, they will be tempted to idealize their style and structure, to confuse it with the will of God, and thus to fail to attend to the movement of the Spirit.

Here is the tension I am exploring. Less-fluid cultures so idealized the institutional church that they treated its material substance as though it was the source of the supernatural power it mediated and sought to represent. That overidentification produced an inflexible resistance to the meaning-making movement of the Spirit. As I will argue later, the emergent church folks get this in spades, and their discourse is full of attacks on the institutional church for this failing. But much of their discussion is naïve if it imagines some self-sustaining network entirely free of institution. I think some form of institution or community structure is necessary and inevitable. Someone must be the webmaster, and even the house church that the emergent folks romanticize has some degree of leadership and organization. So, particularly for those who want to reform rather than replace congregations, the issue is not to do away with structure but to interrogate the structure, asking what old rigidities it defends and pondering what a structure that frees the Spirit would look like.

IMPLICATIONS

The internet, and the forms of virtual community that it enables and encourages, are new developments. Yet, as we live into online connections, they provide a perspective through which we can see more clearly that the church as body of Christ has always been a virtual reality. It connects our experience of God at work in our immediate communities, where we often have immediate bodily connection with sisters and brothers, to a larger conversation with others who are at a distance in time and space. This network ebbs and flows, yet it provides the spaces for embodied folk to think about their experience, connect with embodied others, ceaselessly speak of what God is doing in our varied contexts, and imagine together a faithful future.

DISCUSSION QUESTIONS

- How would you describe your own theology? How has it changed over time? What contributed to that change?
- What is interesting or useful about the suggestion that the church is a network of ceaseless conversation about its belief and practice? What would you add to this definition, or how would you critique it?
- What are the elements of tradition that continue to speak to you, and where do you feel personally and as a congregation called to do a new thing?
- How do you understand the Holy Spirit to be working in your context? How and where is your congregation engaged in new developments that reflect what you understand God to be doing among you? How and where does the congregation miss or resist this conversation about its structure, program, and practice?

7

Beyond Congregations

Church as a series of relationships and communications . . .

This chapter weighs the critique of traditional congregations and denominations that is increasingly heard in digital culture, considers the challenges congregations face today, and looks at alternative forms of Christian community that are emerging. The main ideas here are as follows:

- Established congregations face real challenges. They are less popular and more expensive to maintain. In a shrinking religious marketplace, fewer congregation are needed and not all will survive.
- Their critics see congregations as set in their ways and resistant to more fluid ways of relating. They question congregations' investments in property, hierarchical models of leadership, and firm rules about structure. They report that congregations have expectations they are not sure they want to meet.
- The new forms of Christian community that reflect changes in how people think about religious identity, community, and leadership that are evident are being developed.
- Other innovators are less focused on gathered local communities, instead focusing on building networks of conversation and formation. They seek to leave behind a vision of church defined by fixed congregations and embrace a vision of the church as a network or series of relationships and messages.
- In digital culture, religious leaders are influencers. Their style is more casual, conversational, and rooted in charisma and trust rather than credentials. Often leaders emerge from within the digital conversation, or

from within communities, who do not have traditional credentials such as theological education or ordination.

• When the institutional church is shrinking, and the models of Christian community are changing, there are significant questions about how religious leaders will support themselves. Some religious leaders find other ways to make their work pay, monetizing websites, publishing, or building relationships with other institutions.

The future of religion is contested. When surveyed, many people report no religious affiliation. It is tempting to chalk up the decline in the number people participating in congregational life, and the decline in the number of congregations, to the inevitable rise of a more secular culture. Yet, this is not the whole answer. There is much evidence of spiritual hunger and imagination today. Religion does not seem to be going away. Certainly, congregations are unlikely to win back large numbers of those who no longer claim any religious identity. While the role of organized religion seems to be shrinking, society is also more religiously diverse. There are a variety of online and offline options for those seeking some form of religious community.

One way to describe the situation congregations face is that the market for what they offer is shrinking and becoming more specialized. In the future we are living into, where there are going to be fewer Christians and fewer congregations in the United States, congregations must find their niche. Chapter 8 will give more attention to how congregations can reimagine themselves to be more effective in digital culture. This chapter seeks to understand the contemporary critique of congregations and to look at the alternative forms of Christian community that are emerging even as the number of congregations shrinks.

DO WE NEED CONGREGATIONS?

One challenge that congregations face is that, because religious identity is understood to be personal and individually constructed, increasing numbers of those who have some form of Christian belief and practice do not see congregations as necessary. Many people are seeking forms of spirituality and religious practice and connection that seem less institutional, more personal, and which may be more ephemeral. Church consultant and leadership coach Tom Bandy identifies strengths in these personal, even private, approaches to religious lives. He notes that they can help people go deeper in clarifying their own felt experience of the Holy. They contribute to self-esteem. Because they are not focused on institutions, they are economical and have no environmental footprint. However, he cautions that they can also be self-absorbed, that they rely on personal conscience that is shaped by culture, that they lack accountability and can thus be open to abuse and run the risk of elevating the self to Ultimate Concern.[1] The contemporary focus is on the way individuals construct religious identity. Certainly, many individuals are taking greater personal authority to accept and reject elements of organized religious thought and practice. But there remains a need for some form of shared practice and conversation. What does that look like when many people say they do not find it in congregational life?

There seems to be a split among those seeking to imagine and maintain Christian community between those committed to building new alternative forms of faith community and those who work within the traditional congregations. These groups experience tensions, yet it is not always easy to draw a line between those who are seeking to reform congregations and help them respond to their digital context and others who are ready to leave congregations behind as an outmoded form of religious community. Though there is often distrust, and the two communities do not always communicate well, these groups share a commitment to the idea that Christian faith requires shared practice and connection, and they continue to influence, sometimes support, and often challenge each other. To understand the critiques of congregations that have arisen in digital culture, and to make sense of why digital culture is producing experiments with alternative models of more networked community, it is necessary to recognize this conceptual distinction between more-or-less traditional congregations that are trying to adapt to digital culture and alternative forms of gathering and serving that often exist as an alternative to congregational life.

Is the Institutional Church Part of the Vision?

Some who are thinking about the church's future, particularly people influenced by the emerging church movement that was particularly evident at the turn of the twenty-first century, are critical of what they call the *institutional church.* By institutional, they mean established congregations, whether independent or part of denominations (which are also part of the institutionalization of the church), the sort of congregation that typically meets in a designated sanctuary for weekly worship under the leadership of an ordained pastor. They distinguish the church as an institution, with its organizational structure, rules, and rigidities, from the church as a community of shared practice and belief. They often point to the house churches thought to be typical of the earliest Christians as an expression of the church's ideal form. They seek to build smaller, more flexible, and intimate forms of base Christian community, and many of them use the internet to connect these faith communities and learn from each other's experience. Some go further and imagine opportunities for online community among people who may not be part of a face-to-face gathering.

As described above, though they are united in their concern for building Christian connection and community, there is a history of real and understandable tensions between established congregations and the people experimenting with new forms of a networked faith community. Denominations and congregations that hope to draw on these experiments' energy sometimes sponsor and support new forms of ministry. Their results are mixed. You hear the innovators' frustration in Steven Collins's 2004 discussion of the network the emergent church was building:

> There is no one leader or format or theology, nor is there likely to be. Instead, there is a thriving mess of cross-linkage without regard for conventional church structures or channels of communication. It's the context and lifeblood of the emerging church, . . . yet it's largely invisible to the existing institutional forms of church.

Collins cautions that what the innovators envision will not automatically be subsumed into existing congregations and denominations.

> This is what the institutional church fondly imagines will happen. It sees the emerging forms as parish churches in embryo. . . . Given time, encouragement, resourcing, they will grow the institution, even if it must adapt to new appearances and behaviors.

He imagines there will be some networking with existing forms of church. However, for those creating new models of Christian connection and gathering, networking with denominations and traditional congregations is not necessarily the goal and is sometimes counterproductive.

> This is what is happening. The emerging forms network across and around the institution. Some are connected into it; some are not and maybe don't want to be. Many of them will never be churches in the institutional understanding of the term and attempts at making them so will damage or repel them. They are not so much churches as Church—Church as verb not noun.[2]

If Collins's vision of the church without institution was idealized, the frustration those involved in experimental forms of alternative forms of faith community have with expectations and structures that do not reflect their vision is real. When this happens, more traditional centers of ministry often lose these innovators and experimenters.

Often religious innovation comes from outside the traditional locations of formation and accountability. Access to new media allows emerging leaders to develop a voice and a following without going through traditional and often lengthy systems of formation, certification, or ordination. Denominations and congregations—even those that see the need to innovate and who invest in new forms of Christian community—often struggle to understand and support innovative projects and communities. The Harvard Divinity School project on millennials and religion called *How We Gather*[3] finds the same strained relationship between innovative communities and their denominations that Collins reflected on two decades ago continues today. Those who experiment complain that innovation is treated as something that is valued only after the innovators have fit into traditional boxes. Asked about accurate membership lists or whether they have all the right committees, they become frustrated with their denominations' focus on things that underscore the difference in how they see and measure ministry. Many give up and leave denominations.

There is a real question about whether more traditional congregations and emerging Christian networks, whose visions of the church may differ significantly, can stay in conversation. It will take intentional efforts to keep them in networked conversation about the range of way the church might be faithful within digital culture. It remains to be seen whether they believe they have anything to learn from each other. It may be that they will proceed as parallel movements, advancing or stagnating within narrower conversations.

ALTERNATIVES TO CONGREGATION

What do alternatives to congregations look like? *After Hours, Denver*, the vital experiment in Christian community and service introduced in chapter 1, was launched with "new congregational start" money from the United Methodist Church. Yet, it illustrates why it is hard to decide whether some of these new forms of networked community are or are not congregations. Do *After Hours*, and similar projects, function as congregations, as we have traditionally thought of congregations in the past? Is that what they are striving for? Or does that description create expectations *After Hours* cannot meet and offer a distorted picture of their ministry? We might better understand such projects if we did not expect them to grow into congregations; think of them instead as new interactive models of Christian connection and action. Doing so helps us better understand the religious lives of the people in the different circles that follow *After Hours*. Clarifying our thinking about *After Hours*, and the various other pub theology and dinner church projects, might expand the way we imagine Christian community and challenge our assumptions about what the church can be in a culture of fluid connections.

Practical theologian Pete Ward suggests that the concept of the congregation is outmoded. He writes, "[W]e need to shift from seeing the Church as . . . congregation—to a notion of Church as a series of relationships and communications . . . something like a network or a web rather than an assembly of people."[4] Ward suggests that congregations are too set in their ways to keep up with the flow. Certainly, many congregations will not, and those who do not adapt will struggle to thrive and many will not long survive. Innovators and experimenters experience congregations and denominations as rigid. They find that their commitment to old models of institutional organization and formation stands in the way of trying out new ways of connecting, communicating, and serving. This only increases their conviction that traditional forms of congregation and denomination are not worth the investment. The innovators come to believe that the institutional structures and antiquated vision of denominations and existing congregations block rather than encourage the development of new and more fluid ways of being church.

COMMUNICATING THE GOSPEL: CHRISTIAN IDENTITY, COMMUNITY, AND LEADERSHIP

When people think of communications as only a matter of delivering messages, they imagine that media change simply provides new containers for religious content. When they think in this way, they wrongly imagine that the form of Christianity that they received through the mediation of print culture was an unchanged and unmediated tradition passed down from a pure consensus imagined to exist among the first Christians. In challenging these misunderstandings, I contend that media have always shaped the way people understand themselves and their relationships with each other and with God. Thus, the church's adaptation to digital culture is not simply a matter of whether and how we use digital technologies or gather in online spaces. Those who seek to envision the church for digital culture must understand and respond to the three shifts in religious practice explored in chapters 3, 4, and 5: the renewed focus on the construction of individual religious identity, the development of looser, networked ways of relating, and the development of less hierarchical and formal models of leadership.

Constructing Religious Identity

As described in earlier chapters, oral and written cultures largely understood identity to be something one took from the community as its values, beliefs, and practices were taught by designated leaders. There have of course been challenges to this way of thinking. The rise of modernity and the Protestant Reformation turned the focus to the individual and stressed the guidance of his or her internal moral compass. Digital culture provided a communications system that confirmed this focus on the individual interpreter. Today, people do not simply adopt the practices and assumptions of a particular faith community, accepting it as a package. Instead, they connect to places that make room for their own complexly networked identities. Understanding the way religious identity is constructed today paves the way to understand how increasing numbers of Christians think of themselves and how they then ally with others. Particularly for progressive Christians, religious identity is a mashup. It is constructed from multiple elements, some of which come out of their interaction with culture and other religious traditions. This self is an ongoing project, and no single faith community fully contains it.

What sort of faith communities engage people who think of identity in this way and see the congregation and its tradition primarily as potential resources to be sampled in their private projects of self-exploration? Ward suggests that these folks are seeking a place in a network of "relationships and communications." They want to be invited into a conversation about who they are, and who they want to become. This can happen in both physical and online spaces, where people try on new, richer, more complex understandings of their religious identity. Those attempting to build new forms of religious network respond to these changing desires. They offer the rituals, habits, and beliefs developed within their tradition as resources without signaling that they expect people to accept the whole package. At the same time, they provide a range of ways for people to engage, often around short-term opportunities.

The process of identity formation that these citizens of digital culture are involved in can seem never-ending. For more traditional folk, who assume that the formation and articulation of a clear religious identity *precedes* the practice of faith, it can seem that those focused on their own religious identity will never get on with practices of justice-making, mission, and piety. However, the congregations and communities we have been discussing tend to see Christian identity as something that is built through Christian practice. If that is right, then formation, reflection, and service are simultaneous processes, themselves a mashup out of which emerging identity is tried on or experimented with. Understood in this way, people learn the Christian faith by practicing it, and by having companions who help them reflect on that practice. To make a bolder claim, their practice suggests that it is not right theology that produces clear Christian identity and practice, but that identity and belief grow out of practice.

Identity, Practice, and Social Transformation

While the individual's focus on personal religious identity can be self-absorbed, what many emerging faith communities are discovering is that the search for transformation is not purely personal. People also want to be part of a better world and see the search for that world as part of the clarification and expression of their own identity. Understood in this way, the work of justice and charity is not treated as something that follows formation, but as a place where the church engages people and their spiritual questions.

Consider a couple of examples. On the Colorado plain, at the edge of Aurora, is *The Land* (Thelandumc.org), a five-acre labyrinth leading to a meeting space for worship, community, environmental education, and organizing. There, on Saturdays, people gather to pray and deepen their connection to God in creation. Fifteen miles away, in Denver's Parkhill neighborhood, two congregations who share a building, one Christian and one Jewish, give sanctuary to an undocumented woman and her family as she moves slowly through the process of seeking asylum in the United States. In ways they could not have fully predicted, their commitments to environmental and immigrant justice have become faith practices around which they are articulating new understandings of what God is doing in the world. Whether such projects are organized around concern for the environment, for immigrants, for art and aesthetics, for racial justice, or for serving the homeless, their striving toward religious identity is constantly clarified and tested in practice and worked out in service.

Building Networked Communities

One aspect of digital culture that is changing how Christians connect, communicate, and organize their shared life is the rise of networked relationships. As mentioned in chapter 4, some people make a theoretical distinction between *communities* that are more bounded and tend to be more lasting and *networks* that are looser or more fluid. While the distinction helps us think about the change that is going on around us, it seems more accurate to describe the network as a particular form of community.

Chapter 4 drew on simple diagrams to visualize the difference between the stable congregation and the fluid network. The congregation was represented by a wheel with a clear hub to represent the leaders and built-up traditions that shape the community, spokes that represent the members who relate to the hub, and an outer rim that defined the community's boundaries. It can be hard to break into the community, but it is easy to know who belongs. In contrast, more networked religious communities were represented by two images, a web, and a Venn diagram of overlapping circles. The web points to a multiplicity of relationships, with conversation flowing in multiple directions within the web. There are lots of connections, it is easy to make them, but they are also easily broken. Like the spider's web, it must be maintained and constantly remade. The Venn diagram helps us see that people are not participants in a single web of relationships and communication. They belong to multiple circles each of which has its own focus and often key leaders. Thus, a person's religious life is less likely to be tied to a single community, or tradition, that grows up around a particular leader. They relate to multiple leaders and conversations, and again these relationships are fluid. The Venn diagram is most accurate when we see it as a map of relationships at a particular moment and if we pay attention to how the diagram changes as people build new relationships and/or let others go.

To the extent that congregations idealize stability, seek to be the center of a person's life of faith, and to tie them to a particular theology, tradition, and set of practices, they represent this older, pre-digital way of thinking about the church. Those who seek to reimagine the church as a network are trying to respond to the fluid way of imagining communication and connection that digital culture encourages. In these experimental communities, people come and go. Their network expands as it establishes new links, connects with multiple leaders and conversations, and thus does not have a single clear center. In the network, people follow multiple leaders and conversations. Though the image oversimplifies what these religious networks are doing, you might describe them as being like dating apps. It is easy to connect with a potential congregation and explore the possibility of a relationship, and it is easy to exit, to "ghost" or disappear from the conversation.

Those who understand these changes, whether they are trying to build new sort of religious institutions and networks or to reform existing congregations, recognize the implications. The shift is, and Ward suggests it should be, from seeing the church as primarily defined by fixed congregations to a sense of the church as a series of relationships and messages.

Theologically the shift is from an image of God and our relationship with the sacred as unchanging to creation-centered images of God as one who is doing a new thing, and exodus images of God establishing new relationships and going with us into new places. If the theological extremes are defined by an image of God fixed on a heavenly throne at one end and God everywhere present amid change at the other, a community that is in the wilderness of the exodus and seeking its land of milk and honey is more likely to be helped by theological images on the fluid side of the scale.

Those attempting to build faith communities rooted in this theology and this networked understanding of what community looks like today, offer easy access in (and out)—thus they have few boundaries, they feature short-term opportunities to connect, learn, and serve, they minimize institution and maximize relationship, and provide multiple ways to be involved.

Leadership and Authority

Those seeking to live into new models of church that make sense to people shaped by the assumptions of digital culture must also think about how understandings of leadership are changing. Who holds religious authority? Where does authority come from? What style of leadership is most effective in your particular situation? Understanding how the answers to these questions are changing makes it easier to make sense of the resistance to many traditional forms of religious leadership and to make sense of the changes in relationships between leaders and faith communities today.

Christians have long given a good deal of authority to tradition. "This is the way our ancestors in the faith did it," or "this is what they believed" have been compelling arguments, and leaders often drew authority from their role as interpreters of tradition. This trust in tradition often rested on the assumption that "the Christian tradition" was singular and unified. Recognizing that the church has always existed as a series of experiments and debates requires a new understanding of tradition. Rather than seeing tradition as settled content of belief and practice, the truly orthodox tradition of the church is the "ceaseless speaking to one another" in which local figures and communities define things provisionally and contextually within a networked conversation with Christians in other times and places.

This more fluid sense of tradition makes sense to Christians who are adapting to digital culture. The digital, with its focus on identity construction, puts the emphasis on the future, on what we are becoming, and not on the past. It is less interested in tradition, or perhaps more accurately gives less authority to tradition. Digital culture suggests that neither the little traditions of a congregation nor the larger traditions of denominational heritage or theologies are treated as a package of belief and practice that must be adopted. Rather, they are source material to be sampled, and if they prove useful, integrated into identity and practice. These new experiments in faith community must be motivated by a vision of the future. They are less about where we have been than about where we are going. As suggested in chapter 5, when Moses was asked "Where are you taking us?," he responded with the promise that God is leading them to "a land of milk and honey."

In a changing culture, people also put less trust in the traditional institutional ways of identifying and preparing religious leaders such as seminary education and ordination. These can remain useful ways to clarify the leader's religious identity, deepen their theological clarity, compassion, and insight, and sharpen their vision. But it is the evidence of these qualities and the establishment of relationships of trust rather than the credential that leads people to grant leaders authority. In keeping with the culture of the people they seek to engage, the style of these religious leaders is casual and conversational. If they are pastors or have other roles that grant them hierarchical authority, they are judicious about how they use it. They are managers of what Rowan Williams called the churches' ceaseless speaking to one another.

Those who are seeking new ways of being "church" are often impatient with these old systems of leadership development and question whether they are worth the time and money they require. They fear that these systems are wedded to old ways of understanding the church and may crush alternative visions. They observe that in digital culture it is crucial to have a clear vision and voice and to build a relationship with a community. Thus, charisma and the evidence of spiritual gifts may be more important than credentials. In this system, the relationship is more to the leader than it is to the institution. One of the implications of this change is that it can make it hard for faith communities to adapt and sustain themselves through transitions in leadership.

Another form of leadership that reflects the networked way of relating is the rise of significant religious influencers who may not be leaders of a specific congregation or group, but who are followed by a network of folks. Some of these people come out of and maintain identity within traditional denominational structures. I think of the influence of people like Lutheran pastor Nadia Bolz Weber and Franciscan friar Richard Rohr. Others, like the mom bloggers described in chapter 5, lack the traditional credentials of theological education and ordination. They perform the religious identity they have constructed, often in confessional ways, and share their vision. If people find them trustworthy and their vision compelling, they build a network of followers.

As important as dynamic leaders are, they are not so likely to be granted hierarchical authority. You see this in congregations as well as alternative communities. Lay folk grant less authority to leaders. They imagine them as consultants and counselors, not as directors or bosses. Thus, people retain the authority to shape their own identity and often expect a considerable voice in shaping the life of the community. There must be both shared leadership and a shared vision for such communities to thrive.

Today, leaders may not hold credentials. They may not have a role in a specific local congregation or alternative group. Yet, if people find them trustworthy, if they have charisma and vision, and communicate a compelling image of how God is with us, they build networks of community and conversation around shared experience and vision.

MONEY, VOLUNTEERS, AND HOW LEADERS GET PAID

As leadership becomes more diffuse and less tied to the institutional church, and as denominations and congregations shrink, significant questions arise about how religious communities and institutions will sustain themselves. As people explore alternative ways of being church, it is hard to separate the questions of whether we need and want to own property, and have congregations lead by seminary-trained pastors, from the very real questions of whether we can afford these things. One compelling form of this question is, how will religious leaders support themselves? When fewer people are drawn to belong to religious communities, and those who do give in more transactional ways, how are leaders going to get paid?

Congregational life as we know it is an expensive proposition. Congregations seek to exist for worship, faith development, and to enable the work of charity and justice. Those desired goals led congregations to acquire real estate that must be maintained and to hire well-educated clergy and other professional staff who understandably desire middle-class lifestyles and pensions. These things seemed easy to acquire when the economy was booming and membership rolls were growing. Today, fewer people seek an ongoing life in a congregation, and as we have seen, those who do are less likely to be fully and regularly involved. As congregations shrink, aging buildings put up in boom times increasingly become burdens that suck resources away from mission. At the same time costs of pensions, health insurance, and salaries rise. For many, this has meant sharing the pastor with other congregations or part-time clergy who do other work.

The question of whether congregations, as we have known them, are sustainable stands alongside the question of whether congregations can adapt to meet contemporary religious needs. Together they motivate the desire to find more sustainable forms of Christian community. For those who have borne the cost of preparing for congregational leadership, often taking on significant debt for theological education, as well as for those who hope to lead the church in the future, these are not abstract questions. For some, there are positions in vital congregations with plenty of resources. For many, the option is to lead one or more small congregations whose shrinking membership focuses attention on institutional survival and reduces both the support for a wider mission and desire for professional leadership.

Of course, congregations exist within the wider American financial system. Christian values may shape the choices we make within that system, but we do not live apart from it. The gig economy is an increasingly large feature of the American economy. Many people who once held long-term jobs now do temporary work for corporations, drive for ride services like Uber, and so forth. Other folks are entrepreneurial and launch small businesses from their homes or seek alternative career paths. Not surprisingly, this is increasingly a part of emerging models of ministry.

As there are fewer opportunities to lead congregations, and as increasing numbers of people who experience a call to some form of ministry doubt that congregations are the best place to live out that calling, they turn to other forms of ministry. Chaplaincy, whether in hospitals, colleges, prisons, or the military provides opportunities for ministry that are focused on pastoral care and which may be tied to institutions with more financial resources. Other religious leaders have responded to the dissatisfaction with congregational life and the focus on personal religious identity by developing coaching and mentoring skills that allow them to companion individuals in their development of religious identity. The boom in spiritual direction and the long-term growth in faith-oriented counselors reflects this. We see both conservative and progressive expressions of these adaptations to more individualized religious identities. Still others enter more directly into digital culture as bloggers and authors of spiritual or self-help books.

For some, these alternative forms of ministry supplement a leadership role in a specific congregation. For others, they are a way to leave congregational leadership behind, often by building a wider networked audience or market. Whether located within congregations or functioning as entrepreneurs, they primarily support the work of developing and clarifying personal religious commitments and practices.

As congregations struggle and some of those trained as religious professionals turn to other forms of ministry, the role of volunteer lay leadership becomes increasingly important. Some small congregations are becoming largely lay led, and many of the new forms of Christian community are being developed by volunteers and bi-vocational pastors. How should people who care about the church think about these changes? Some of the changes we see reflect the decline of many congregations. Sadly though, as congregations shrink, their spiritual and financial resources often decline. Too often they become entirely inwardly focused, losing sight of their wider mission, and their pastor's role narrows to that of a chaplain who provides care through the period when individuals and the institution are dying. Yet, size need not be the only measure of success. There are vital small congregations where people are reimagining ministry in a digital culture where fewer people will identify as Christian. This change may not always be good news for people who want to build careers as pastors or teachers of pastors. There are not as many of those jobs as there once were. Those who are successful in guiding the church through this transition will need a new vision and new skills.

CONCLUSION

I expect there will continue to be vital brick-and-mortar congregations. However, assuming that they are the only or best form of shared Christian life can blind us to what else is emerging. Further, existing congregations cannot expect that those building new styles of Christian community will reach out to them. If congregations and their leaders want to be part of these alternative networks, they need to better understand the vision of the church that motivates experimenters and build conversations that include them.

Today, the congregation is but one of the multiple ways people envision a Christian community. Some people do not find congregations to be the most helpful place to work on their Christian self-understanding and shape their practice. They turn to different visions of community and formation. They may seek the structure and support of twelve-step groups, participate in short-term spiritual retreats or service projects, or develop online relationships with religious bloggers and their followers. For those who care about congregations and hope they will have vital futures, it is both liberating and frightening to recognize that there are other forms of Christian community. Our congregations are but some of the experiments with Christian community.

DISCUSSION QUESTIONS

- How does your congregation reflect the problems that are described in the chapter? Do these challenges suggest that your congregation needs to reframe its vision and practice, change its structure and program, try new things or reconsider its viability? What elements of its life make your congregation a vital center and what challenges does it face?
- Are you aware of alternative forms of ministry or new congregational starts in your community? Who do they seem to attract? How is their life different from that of your congregation? What might you learn from them?

- Could your congregation launch or support an alternative form of ministry that might create a faith community for new people? If so, what would it look like?

8

Reforming Congregations

Church without the parts that suck . . .

This concluding chapter urges congregations to adopt a lived theology that sees God in the fluidity of digital culture. It describes six steps or locations for the work of adapting to that culture:

- Embrace network thinking
- See and assess your congregation and its context
- Clarify your vision
- Welcome without expectation
- Build networked communication
- Create program and decision-making systems that support and expand your network

Congregations face big challenges. Demographics show a steady decline in numbers, visitors say they feel either unwelcome or overwhelmed, and many who want to re-envision Christian community find us too slow to change. One year, folks from *After Hours* carried a banner in Denver's Gay Pride Parade proclaiming, "*After Hours, Denver*, it's like church without the parts that suck!" They sought to catch the attention of folks who are suspicious of the institutional church yet want spiritual companions and conversation. Can congregations take these folks on their own terms, make room for their doubts and questions, and provide resources for their spiritual work?

The rise of networks helps explain why many religious seekers don't find what they are looking for in traditional congregations. However, it is not only those outside the institutional church whose religious desires and expectations are shaped by digital culture. It is likely that people already in your congregation see their religious identity as a personal construction, desire looser and more networked ways of relating, and respond better to less hierarchical, more informal models of leadership. Adapting to these changing expectations can revitalize a congregation's internal life as well as opening the doors to new folks.

Congregations that want to change must ask those who have walked away, "What sucks about congregations?" I believe that a large measure of what sucks about congregational life is the hierarchy, boundaries, and rigidity that tie congregations to a fading culture. Today, these are distractions from the search for a faith experience that transforms and illumines people's lives and world. When we who are engaged in congregations let go of the rigid residue of past cultural forms and find more fluid ways to relate, it's easier to see the new things the Spirit is doing. This change is hard, yet some congregations have not given up. They believe that their shared life can be richer in digital culture, that they have something to offer, and they seek to make it accessible.

Live into a Theology of Networked Community

Our "lived theology" is the set of assumptions about God, humans, culture, and the church that are implicit in the way we live. It may be different than our professed theology. The changes in how Christians connect, communicate, and organize their shared life that digital culture encourages suggest a different lived theology than is implicit in more fixed understandings of the church. Chapter 4 contrasted the stable congregation's boundaries, expectations, and one-way communication with the fluid network's easy access, limited expectation, and conversations that flow in multiple directions. Congregations that idealize stability, assume they are the center of a person's life of faith, and impose a singular doctrine and set of practices represent this older pre-digital way of thinking about the church. If your congregation only imagines God and your experience of the sacred as fixed and unchanging, they will resist change.

Coming to see the church as "a network of relationships and messages" within which people engage God and God's people reflects a theological shift. This is not just a different way of thinking about what people do, but about how God is with us. Here, creation is ongoing; God leads an exodus toward a new way of being church. Such lived theologies invite curiosity. Questions of faith and differences in understanding are accepted as part of the discovery of individual and congregational identity. This theological openness invites relational openness. It seems natural to network with lots of people with differing beliefs and practices and to let them control their level of involvement.

Why Weak Ties Matter

It may seem counterintuitive to invest so much attention in people who don't seem interested in establishing deep relationships with your congregation. Chapter 4 discussed the sociological evidence that relationships are established and maintained by both strong and weak ties. Think of the ways that social courtesies establish weak but real connections in the line at the grocery store or how a neighborhood cleanup project or 4th of July picnic connects neighbors who don't otherwise know each other. In a similar way, openness and welcome, whether they lead to new members or not, expands the congregation's connections and impact on its community.

In less fluid times, people built lasting relationships with institutions. Families might belong to the same congregation for generations. Today, those ties are weaker; you are more likely to have a complex network of connections to a variety of people and institutions. A focus on individual identity narrows our attention to the parts of the congregation's life that match our commitments and interests. To be effective in such a culture, your congregation needs relationships with a larger number of people. It is tempting for those with long ties to the congregation to treat this lower level of investment as a personal failing on the part of new folks who are doing "less than they should." Instead, recognize this as a cultural pattern that is common in a networked society. This shifts the focus from "what is wrong with them," to "what can we do to open up our internal network, so access is easier?"

Of course, decisions must be made, money raised and managed, and programing planned. This requires that some people with strong ties to the congregation make larger and longer commitments. Eventually you will build stronger ties with some of the folks in your network, but only if you don't push them away by asking more time and attention than they are ready to invest. Invite, but don't insist.

BECOMING CONGREGATIONS THAT DON'T SUCK

Below are six steps your congregation can take to develop a more fluid and flexible faith-based practice that makes it more efficient and effective. Treat this as a buffet; some things will not be appropriate for your congregation. In deciding where to start, you might pick a couple of projects that would be easy to accomplish. Success builds confidence. Also consider something harder but that holds out the promise to be transformational.

1. Embrace Networked Thinking

Perhaps the hardest barrier to overcome is that pre-network ways of thinking are baked into the DNA of most of our congregations. Designed as stable traditional communities, they have clear insider/outsider boundaries and expect levels of commitment and investment that it takes years of relationship to develop. In return, insiders feel known and affirmed. It is difficult for them to see the things that make it hard for newcomers to break in and for the congregation to adapt to cultural change.

Networked thinking leads you to think of your congregation in new ways. As discussed more fully in chapter 4, "Connections in Communities and Networks," this shifts our focus from boundaried relationships and identities defined by tradition toward the more fluid relationships typical of digital culture. Chapter 6, "A Brief Theology of the Church as Network" pointed to theological implications of this way of thinking about the church, relationships, and identity. Attention to fluidity, construction, and change draws attention to the ongoing work of the Holy Spirit as a primary way of thinking about how God is with us amid change.

Networked thinking encourages both strong and weak ties. It constantly makes new connections, encourages multiple voices, and doesn't worry if some of them are fleeting. This expands the congregation's connections and shifts its focus from structures and programs that assume long-term connections to those that gather people around immediate interests and concerns. There participants learn from each other's practice of faith, come to know neighbors, invite people into the congregation's online and physical spaces, and create or publicize opportunities for service. The internal ties may not be as strong, but by building relationships with other individuals, congregations, community groups, and religious leaders, the networked congregation is constantly renewed by fresh interactions and insights.

This way of thinking becomes a yardstick to measure every element of your congregation's life. Whether analyzing your existing strengths and challenges, identifying the wider network you might be a part of, working on welcome, evaluating worship and other programs, or developing new ministries and missions, you ask, "How do we lower the boundaries to involvement, expand our conversations, and extend our networks of connection and commitment?"

To expand their networks, congregations "friend" individuals and groups who may not become regular participants in worship. Progressive Lutheran pastor Nadia Bolz-Weber says, "to build a network you have to 'like' a lot of people and hope they will 'like' you back."[1] This is in part a metaphor for networked thinking, but she also means it literally. Include links on your own and your congregations' websites to leaders you admire, like-minded congregations, and community groups. Hopefully, some will reciprocate, and this will increase your online flow of people and information. Thus, you expand your visibility and the size of the network, even if the links are not strong.

Most congregations will have elements of both traditional and networked community. The goal in embracing networked thinking is not to drive out the strong ties built over time, but to avoid signaling that they are a requirement for involvement. If you have existing long-term fellowship groups that are meeting a need, you don't abandon them. You do need to recognize that they are hard to break into. To open your network, put your energy into short-term topical programs that bring varied people together.

2. Assess Your Congregation and Context

Begin by asking what those already involved like about your congregation and where they see things that no longer seem to work. What vision of the church seems to motivate the congregation? What are the things that enrich your shared life, and what blocks you? Who gets heard and who gets silenced in congregational conversation and decision making? What are the official and unofficial ways that decisions get made or blocked? Can you build on your strengths? What changes will enrich your shared life? From there you can turn to the harder question of whether aspects of the congregation that work for insiders also appeal to the people you are trying to attract. Questionnaire A in appendix 1 provides a list of questions to help focus this assessment.

To open your congregation's network and build relationships with more people, you need to identify who they are, what they want, and how they see your congregation. It is hard for insiders to see the congregation as others do. It helps to talk with neighbors and visitors or draw on consultants to get a sense of how they experience your congregation. Census data illuminates the community where you are located. Who is out there and what do they need and desire?

Knowing your neighbors helps you consider how the congregation might change to meet their needs. Do you open your building to community groups; do church leaders attend public meetings? If you are not building links with neighbors, what boundaries and barriers are limiting those connections? Partnering with ecumenical and interfaith groups or with community organizations is one expression of the desire for wider networks. Hosting a League of Women Voters' candidates' night, participating in community efforts to address homelessness, or sharing in acts of public mourning or celebration all build and make visible your web of relationships. Questionnaire B in appendix 1 provides a list of questions to help focus this conversation.

One challenge for struggling congregations is that their palpable need often repels the people they want to attract. As noted in chapter 1, "Christian Life in Media Culture," anxiety about the future leads congregations to expect newcomers to solve the congregation's problems by taking on ways of relating that were typical in the past. However, a desire to rescue the institution is not what draws visitors, and these implicit expectations often drive them away. If you identify, explore, and manage your anxieties and expectations, you are better able to welcome those who may want to sample what you have to offer.

One key strategic question is whether your congregation sees a need for change. It is almost certainly the case that not everyone agrees. How will you find allies, open conversations about what change might look like, and manage resistance? While it is important to build shared understanding and support for change, you may never come to complete consensus. At some point, those who see the need for change must begin to strategize and begin the work.

Assess your leadership resources.

The ways people's expectations of leaders are changing in digital culture is discussed in chapter 5, "Leadership and Authority." It will help you think about how the role and style of leaders are changing in digital culture. It also addresses the cultural desire for charismatic leaders who bring vision and the need for leaders who lead processes of developing shared vision for congregations that want to be more effective in digital culture.

People desire two conflicting things from leaders. On the one hand, they are drawn to dynamic leaders who articulate a vision that shapes the community's conversation. On the other hand, people focused on personal religious identity resist being told what to do and want a more level system where leadership is shared. There must be shared leadership and vision for a new congregational culture to develop and thrive.

No leader has every skill. You need to identity the gifts, capacity, and commitments of clergy and lay leaders; think about how to make the best use of them. What are their limits for the work ahead? Are they open to change, or do they resist it? Are they charismatic leaders who draw people to a compelling vision of what the church can become? Are they program builders or pastoral care providers? Where will you need to turn to others in the congregation or consultants for assistance?

Whether it is megachurch pastors like Joel Osteen or online opinion leaders like Diana Butler Bass and Richard Rohr, charismatic leaders gather networks of followers. Those drawn to them want to feel they know the leader, to see his or her religious identity, experience their theological clarity, compassion, and insight. It is often these qualities, and the establishment of relationships of trust, rather than a sense of institutional belonging, that draw people. In this sense, having a charismatic, visionary, and relational pastor is particularly helpful as congregations struggle with change.

Yet, as people become involved, they resist old hierarchical models of leadership and seek a voice in shaping the congregation's vision and ministry. At this stage, the congregation needs a leader who manages conversation about what the congregation is becoming. The leader may mask her own vision to allow a consensus to emerge. These leaders may be less charismatic but better at building systems and processes. Though some leaders will be more visionary and others better at process, the best congregational leaders balance these seemingly conflicting desires and seek help from others in the areas where they less focused or gifted.

3. Clarify Your Vision

To get where you want to go, your congregation needs an easily communicated vision of who you are and where you are headed. Sometimes a compelling metaphor arises that guides the congregation. One Chicago congregation, struggling to recover after a fire destroyed their building, was captured by a sermon on Jesus's parable of the sower who scattered seed, some falling on fallow ground but some on good ground that bore fruit. Whether they were discouraged by setbacks or celebrating accomplishments, someone would remind them that they were spreading the seeds from which something new would eventually spring forth.

Chapter 1, "Life in Media Culture," chapter 5, "Leadership and Authority," and chapter 6, "A Brief Theology of the Church as Network" each help you think about your vision. When the past has less authority, vision serves as a road map. A clear vision that expresses values and direction helps people see why they should be attracted to your congregation.

Vision is clarified in conversations about your context and hopes. The process might start with leaders beginning to articulate a proposal. It could begin, or be further developed, in a small group or committee. They might work on a draft or plan a process for wider congregational conversation to build consensus and support. Questionnaire C in appendix 1 provides questions to get you started. The end product may be a formal mission/vision statement or a more informal consensus that helps you focus your actions. You may find it helpful to develop both a longer working document and a sentence or two of summary that you can easily share and refer to. Imagine something that can serve as a hashtag.

Vision and mission grow out of (1) your assessment of the strengths and challenges of the congregation, (2) the needs and desires of the community where you serve, (3) your understanding of what works in digital culture, and (4) the Spirit's movement in your context. Thus, your congregation's vision must be more focused than the broader mission and vision of the church in every time and place. If your statement says something like "Our church seeks to express the love of God in the world," you need to dig deeper. What does it mean for this congregation, with its unique gifts and limits, to express God's love? Who are the people you are realistically seeking to engage and serve with? How will you connect with them and build networks of relationship? What are the concrete signs that would make God's love evident in the places where you will serve?

Think about scale.

Changing visions of the church and a revitalized view of what the Spirit is doing in your congregation can be exciting. Yet, the economic realities created by declining numbers are often discouraging. The earlier that your congregation begins to analyze its context and resources and to strategize about what forms its ministry will take, the more likely it is that you will still have the imaginative and financial resources to find new life.

One answer to these challenges has been for congregations to get bigger. Megachurches are, in part, a creation of digital culture. They recognize the appeal of celebrities in digital culture and have learned the lesson of economic scale. Seeing how big digital retailers have grown, they build a wide network, which tends to drive out smaller, less-efficient competitors. They put on a good show and don't ask much of those who attend. By offering easy access to an array of appealing messages and services, they often function as an inwardly focused network. This meshes with aspects of digital culture we have been talking about but in a more commercialized way that often reflects and encourages the "prosperity gospel" proposed by preachers like Joel Osteen and T. D. Jakes.

Smaller to mid-sized congregations have fewer resources and need a different strategy, one that is both more flexible and more focused. They can't be all things to all people and must consider who they are trying to reach. This is often counterintuitive. Anxiety about membership decline increases the sense that they want to reach everybody. But in digital culture, people comparison shop, seeking out the congregation that best matches their needs and identity. Thus, the path forward requires honest conversations about who you want to attract and what distinguishes you. For some people, a smaller congregation is better.

Your vision is not a clear blueprint of the finished project but a directional pointer. It communicates to outsiders what is distinctive about your congregation, helps focus your decision making, and shapes your priorities. In all your communications (preaching, blogging, the congregation's website, in community meetings, and so on), you then explore these distinctive claims about God and what God is doing among you, discuss why they matter, and together create new ways of relating, worshiping, and serving that move you toward your vision.

4. Welcome without Expectations

I have never visited a congregation that didn't think they were welcoming. Yet, many visitors feel ignored and find it hard to break in. Understandably, insiders are focused on their own interactions, and it is easy to exclude new-comers. Other visitors feel overwhelmed by expectations. Welcome seems tied to rushing them into ongoing commitments, to connecting them to groups and classes, to considering membership, and so they withdraw and don't return. Chapter 4 "Connections in Communities and Networks" and chapter 7, "Beyond Congregations" give more in-depth attention to how shifting expectations about how people will connect to congregations complexifies the questions of inclusion and expectation. Congregations that want to attract people are well advised to give attention to visitors' experience and strive to up the welcome and lower the expectation. This builds your network in ways that allow people to participate on their own terms.

There are techniques for welcoming visitors. It is likely that you have received advice from other sources about removing barriers for people who show up for worship. Is the building accessible? Are visitors greeted by insiders who take an interest in them? Are there robust systems of follow-up? Do your website, signs, and other publicity provide clear information about worship time, Sunday school and childcare, and social hour? These steps make access easier.

It is also important to consider whether your welcome is conditional. Is it rooted in traditional assumptions about building up membership and consistent participation? To expanding your network and welcoming people on their own terms requires warmth without expectation. Your first message is, "Welcome, we are interested in you, come as often as you would like." Later, if they show interest, there will be opportunities to offer places to connect and grow. Again, the message is "You are welcome to try any of them on and see if they fit."

Why is it so hard to get welcome right? Partly, because people want different things. Some visitors are extroverts ready to stand up in worship and introduce themselves, while introverts hate such focused attention. Well-intended insiders may push too hard or lose focus on new folks as they attend to their existing relationships. But there are harder reasons, particularly for congregations in diverse or changing neighborhoods. It is easy to welcome people who are like us and have similar expectations of what church will be like. If the racial makeup, social class, or age curve of your neighborhood is changing, visitors may have different expectations. Welcome may require you to think about whether the style of worship, music, and preaching speak to potential newcomers. It takes awareness and work to welcome difference.

Finally, welcome is an ongoing process. Do you have programs that are easy to join and that welcome occasional visitors? Are small groups and committees accessible and inviting? Do they think about how to include people without overwhelming them? Are there opportunities for people who are showing up to participate in conversations about the vision and direction of your congregation? How easy is it to move into leadership?

5. Embrace networked communications

Pete Ward suggests that in an information age the church is best understood as a series of messages and relationships.[2] The digital is both a metaphor that teaches a new approach to religious identity and networked relationships *and* an actual system of communication. It is increasingly important to use it well. The discussion of how changes in media are related to shifts in how people think about religious identity and practice, is in chapter 1, "Christian Life in Media Culture" and chapter 2, "Church in American Media Culture." The discussion of our current digital culture in chapter 4, "Connections in Communities and Networks," extends this and invites you to think about both the communications systems your congregations uses and the expectations about identity, community, and leadership that they encourage.

When the internet first arose, people thought of it as a print shop and a library. Congregations compose bulletins and newsletters on computers, email announcements about worship and other opportunities to gather, and digitize financial records. A simple website served as a sort of billboard to make the congregation more visible. These were good first steps, but they treat the internet as merely a faster version of print culture's one-way communication system and see the congregation's online presence as a support system for the "real ministry" that happens offline.

The internet is more than a source of information about your congregation's programs. As became clearer during the COVID-19 pandemic, the network is a space within which we can gather to worship, hold meetings, or receive pastoral and spiritual care.[3] As congregations got better at these things, the online space became an open forum for conversation.

What has your congregation learned about the possibility for religious life in digital spaces from its COVID-19 experience? For some congregations, the pandemic pushed their life entirely online for a period, and a "return to normal" is likely a relief. Yet, online worship and fellowship have connected them to people who don't come into the building. Many are thinking about how to maintain those relationships in the future by continuing some form of streaming worship. They ask which meetings and gathering are best done face-to-face and which might better be done online. This increased hybridity is likely to be one of the pandemic's lasting effects on Christian practice.

Networked space is a kind of public square. Information flows through the network in every possible direction. Everyone is a node who can receive, block, and send messages. People shaped by their experience of digital culture expect to be part of a conversation. Because of this openness, information easily flows in and out of the networked congregations. When someone reposts the pastor's sermon, tweets, or comments on Facebook about your congregation, their network becomes an extension of your network.

Social media forums are not easily controlled by the pastor or parish office. This openness challenges leaders' desire for communications to flow from them to followers. To get the full benefits of the network, you must overcome this resistance and embrace a style of communications that invites feedback and conversation. Responding to the desire for more open communication will require setting norms about what is appropriate and monitoring the congregation's website. Often, this can be managed by coaching the conversation; from time to time it will be necessary to confront or take down inappropriate posting.

Considering how information flows within your congregation will help you to think about how fully your congregation embraces or resists the logic of networks. Do you use social media primarily to amplify the one-way flow of information? Or, embracing the logic of the network, does your congregation see the internet as a space for meeting and conversation? Where are the strong voices, what on- and offline conversations are they inviting, or cutting off, and how do others break in? How and where is your congregation part of wider conversations about the nature of the faith, its best practices, and implications for the life of the wider community?

Can people see what is special about your congregation?

Those seeking congregations have lots of choices. How will the people who "ought" to like you find you? Some of this is informal. As you adopt a more networked identity, people in your network will "like" the congregation, comment on it in their own social media, creating links that make it visible. There are also more formal places to connect with the congregations. Whether it's your website, social media, a leader's blog or newsletter, or hosting community events, you want some consistent places people can expect to find you. The vision statement should then shape the messages you want to put out; it says "This is who we are." You don't have to be on every social media platform but be reliably present. Similarly, you don't have to express an opinion on every topic. Have a clear and consistent message that engages the people with whom you want to be in conversation. Focus on key commitments where you have capacity, expertise, and passion. This helps you stand out in the vast marketplace of congregations that are out there.

6. Create Program and Decision-Making Structures That Support Networked Relationships

People complain that congregational structures are bureaucratic, that they impede rather than enable ministry and that small group structures seem to lock people into long-term commitments. In some ways this is not a new complaint, but the fluid ways that people connect, communicate, and build relationships described in chapter 4, "Connections in Communities and Networks," explain why they are particularly pressing today. Chapter 7, "Beyond Congregations," looks at the way that they drive innovators out of congregations and make newer folks anxious about engaging. It is worth asking whether this way of life serves or impedes your mission. Can people become involved without becoming overwhelmed?

Formation and religious education for transitory people.

Practical theologian Katherine Turpin tells the story of a family loosely related to the congregation where she worships who brought their children to Sunday school for a year, then the next year opted for the formative experience of youth soccer. What, she wonders, does religious formation look like when people come and go so freely? She notes that the Sunday School model assumes that the best way to engage is for fifty minutes a week over a long time and wonders whether that is working today.[4]

With Turpin, you might ask whether old models of long-term religious education continue to be effective. The church has a long history of offering shorter term intense formative experiences. Spiritual retreats and summer camp are traditional expressions of this approach. In Colorado, a project called *Judaism Your Way* seeks to bring people with Jewish ties, but who are not part of a synagogue, together around ritual moments. Their mission is to provide innovative opportunities to connect Jewishly through affirming, welcoming, inclusive, and responsive low-barrier experiences. In this way, *Judaism Your Way* offers an alternative, an open tent, for people to gather and experience the rich tapestry of Judaism in a spirit of freedom and acceptance.[5]

"Alternative," "low-barrier," and "affirming" capture something of what people are seeking as they consider relating to religious communities. Replacing or supplementing long-term forms of formation with intense short-term "open tent" experiences is a way for your congregation to invest in spiritual seekers who may become part of your network even if they aren't regular participants.

Seeing your congregation as a network raises questions. Is it easy to get involved, and can people control the level of commitment they need to make? Deciding to participate in a class, committee, or social group that has no obvious end point requires a level of commitment that traditional congregations desire. This may not be the relationship newer people are looking for. The barriers are lower if the congregation offers a buffet of short-term opportunities to connect people.

Decision-making systems that give permission.

Who is in charge, how do you plan and make decisions, and do these processes serve you well? Every congregation has formal systems to manage its life. Clergy, elected officers, and boards or committees have power. The congregation also has informal systems. Some people, by their style of engagement, history with the congregation, or resources, have huge influence. Either or both systems may be healthy or unhealthy. They can be locations for vision and innovation, or they can block needed changes. Understanding these systems helps innovators find allies, identify sticking places, and consider where reform is needed. Because traditional communities tend to value and reward longevity, it is often the case that leadership systems that resist networked ways of thinking perpetuate themselves. In thinking about your congregation, look at the formal and informal systems, ask who holds power within them, and how leaders are selected. Do the same people continue to hold power, and how do they use it?

One recurring complaint is that congregations have too many layers of decision making. There are two key problems with this: first, it puts the emphasis on the institution and frustrates people who want to spend their time in ministry not in planning; secondly it often serves to discourage innovation and change. Administrative meetings expand to fill the time you give them. How many committees, boards, and other decision makers do you have? Do they invite innovation and serve your mission, or do they keep leadership in the hands of longtime members?

An approach sometimes called "adhocracy" seeks to limit the size and number of standing committees and to give permission to innovate to small often short-term groups of people who gather around particular programs, missional commitments, or fellowship groups. There are two goals here: first, to speed up decision-making processes and give permission and support as often as possible to people ready to try new things; secondly, to narrow the range of responsibility and the length of the commitment so that busy people find places to experiment with stronger ties and deeper participation in the congregation.

We should touch on how congregations raise money. Once, you could set a budget and people pledged to support the whole program. Single folks and the elderly supported programs for children and families as an investment in the long-term health of the congregation. This happens less today. Transitory people are less comfortable making a long-term pledge; they want the opportunity to give to support ministries that meet their needs or express their values. They also expect to pay for services they receive. To longtime givers, this seems unfaithful, but you can expand the web of support of the congregation if you offer an array of ways for people to give.

Of course, a congregation needs some structure, a way to develop vision and make shared decisions. The question is, how much? If it feels like you spend more time in meetings than in ministry, strive for the smallest amount of long-term structure you need to maintain your life as a community and institution. Ask yourself, are there elements of your structure that no longer serve you well and places where you can create more and shorter opportunities for a wider web of people to participate, serve, and lead?

Rethink how and where you meet.

Some congregations are reimagining the way they meet and serve in more radical ways. These changes may not be right for your congregation, but seeing how people are experimenting can enliven your ability to imagine new forms that your congregation might take or help launch.

Change isn't easy. It requires that you challenge often unexplored assumptions, that some people let go of power—or have it taken from them—so that new visions, different habits, and fresh ways of relating can take hold. Many congregations cannot or do not really want to change. You see this in congregations in racially changing neighborhoods. They want to build networks in the community and welcome people from the new group, but they resist the call to give up power or change their familiar practices. In such cases it may be more helpful to launch new parallel programs in the church building or other places in the community.

Should you shake up where and how you gather?

Some congregations who simultaneously maintain a traditional sanctuary are also experimenting with gathering in more public places. To signal that they are not "your grandparents' church," they sometimes meet in bars for "pub theology." Similar gatherings happen in coffee shops or other public places. Rather than asking new folks to come to them, these congregations go where people gather. The invitation is "Come, grab a drink, listen to a discussion starter, and join in the conversation." They often include some version of sharing joys and concerns and prayer. The barriers to participation are very low, and people are comfortable coming once, erratically, or regularly.

"Dinner church" is an effort to build a more sustained small group with stronger ties. Modeled on the house church, they typically gathered for a shared meal. Though they may sing, and incorporate other structures of worship, they also tend to reduce the distinction between worship, teaching, and conversation. In some ways they seem like more established prayer or fellowship groups. However, they tend to be less pious, to make more room for doubt, and to welcome people wherever they may be in constructing a religious identity. Congregations with low barriers to involvement actively welcome people into these groups whether they are otherwise involved in the congregations or not. Like pub theology gatherings, they often attract people who don't come to the sanctuary.

Should you find a different relationship to space?

Asking questions about how people want to gather, and assessing what your congregation can afford, raises other questions about buildings and property. Is yours a congregation with a large, expensive-to-maintain, building designed for ministry in a different era? For some these legacy spaces are themselves a resource that attracts people and it makes sense to find ways to support them. For others, the obligation to support a building that no longer meets their needs limits their possibilities. The pastor of a now small and largely older urban congregation, whose building includes a large sanctuary and a gym, says he jokes that if someone sees smoke they should wait until the fire is raging to call the fire department. He believes that the burden of maintaining the building crushes the congregation's sense of wider mission, that being free of it would allow the congregation to think more creatively about what forms of worship they wanted and free them to serve their community in new ways.

There is no single right answer about congregational property and space. Some urban congregations, where land is valuable, have sold off the airspace above their traditional buildings or formed partnerships with developers that give them space in commercial skyscrapers that replace the original building.[6] Some are creating partnerships with other congregations, schools, or agencies to share the use and cost of their buildings. Some are questioning whether the ministries they imagine require them to own and maintain property. They find it more flexible to gather in rented or borrowed spaces. Still others are developing more complex relationships to the earth and environment. For some this means urban farms, a labyrinth in the yard, or attention to how they use energy.

REIMAGINING CHRISTIAN LIFE AND CONNECTION

Consider the sort of messages and connections your congregation is trying to share. When I was in seminary, my theology professor compared two church buildings. One was a European cathedral that had stood for a thousand years, the other a Midwestern sanctuary designed so that, if the congregation failed, it could easily be converted to a warehouse. He contrasted the grandeur of the vision of the church and the theological conviction of the people who built a sanctuary to stand for millennia with what he saw as the pragmatism and anxiety of those who saw the church as an experiment that might not work out. But looking back from our networked and fluid location, one might frame this differently. Perhaps the midwestern congregation is not so much planning for failure as living out of a theology of fluidity and change in which the Holy Spirit is always ready to do a new thing among God's people.

Because digital culture is about constructing something new, it is focused on the future. Congregations seeking to be the church today embrace what the Spirit is doing, articulate a vision, and expand their networks to become spaces where people explore and articulate Christian identity and find new ways of serving. Welcome to the journey of discovery!

DISCUSSION QUESTIONS

- Does your congregation need to make changes to adapt to digital culture and networked thinking? Why, or why not? What do you see as the easiest changes to make? What would be the most crucial steps?

- What questions does the chapter raise about your vision of the church and your congregation's mission? How would you like to see the vision and mission clarified and/or refocused?
- Is your congregation welcoming? Are worship and other programming easy to access? What barriers might visitors experience? What could you do about them?
- How does your congregation communicate with participants? Is the flow of information one way or does it invite response and multiple voices? Is it visible in the wider community? Does it create conversation with the wider community? How does it do these things? What changes would invite more open and networked relationships?
- Are your administrative and decision-making systems clear and efficient? Do they welcome and support innovation? Are they slow to make decisions and resistant to change? Are newer people invited into leadership? What changes would make the congregation's systems more effective, less time-consuming, and more supportive of new ministries?

Questionnaires for Congregational Planning Discussions

Below are three questionnaires or discussion guides designed to help groups within your congregation (A) think through and analyze the character, strengths, and challenges of the congregation, particularly those that arise within digital culture; (B) analyze your surrounding community, clarify who your neighbors are, identify their needs and desires, gifts, and challenges, and pondering how your context clarifies your mission; and (C) clarify and articulate the congregation's mission and vision. Your *mission* is a matter of your congregation's identity and faith commitments, of who you serve, and how you do it. Your *vision* is a picture of where you are going. It identifies your hopes and the problems you are solving and clarifies who you want to network with and how you want to make your congregation, the larger church, and the world better.

This process invites you to begin by asking what you like about the congregation, to tease out where you may be frustrated by its shared life, and to think about what would enrich your experience. From there, you will think about how cultural change and the needs and desires of people you would like to attract might invite new ways of relating. Some of these questions will be more important in your situation than others. Feel free to adapt them to your needs.

Though even shorter conversations about these things, which might happen in an adult education setting, congregational board meeting, or a retreat are helpful, this work takes time. Larger congregations might spend as much as a year to eighteen months working toward shared understanding, a clear vision statement, and a plan for implementing it. In small congregations, the process can move more quickly.

Think about who should be involved in planning. Those who hold church offices and people who volunteer in various areas of ministry (Sunday school teachers, worship planners, youth workers, and mission volunteers, etc.) seem obvious. Also, include people from different age and racial groups, and make sure that both women and men are involved. It is particularly helpful to have some newer people, they often bring fresh insight about things that are no longer evident to longtime participants. You might begin with informal conversations about selected questions. You may be at a stage where more formal surveys and studies of the congregation are helpful; or a focused retreat gathering can be a helpful way to advance this sort of self-study.

Small congregations, say less than seventy-five to one hundred members, are likely to proceed informally. They are less likely to produce formal mission and vision statements or to find them helpful. Still, conversation that clarifies and builds consensus about their identity, their location in wider communities, and their mission and vision are helpful. Larger congregations are likely to be better served by more formal processes that lead to clear vision statements and goals.

QUESTIONNAIRE A: ANALYZING THE CONGREGATION

1. *Describe your congregation's distinctive character and culture.* What is unique about your congregation? What does it do well? Is there a shared theology? Is a particular denomination or a movement like the emergent church community or evangelicalism part of your identity and network? Does your congregation embrace, resist, or reshape the practices and habits of those wider faith communities? What programs, service groups, or social groups do you have? Do they attract people to the congregation? Describe your congregation's style, level of formality, and distinctive shared habits. Are you a neighborhood church or do people from other areas seek you out? Do you have digital connections with people who are not likely to attend physical gatherings? Do you have connections with the surrounding community? Do you participate in ecumenical groups or community organizations, host voting, have a food pantry, or in other ways engage with your neighbors? Are there ways in which you wish it would change? Are changes needed to attract new people?

2. *What is your worship life like?* What are the music, preaching, and liturgy like? What are the recurring messages and themes in your services? What are the familiar elements of worship? Are there sometimes surprising activities or messages? Do you primarily watch and listen

or are you active? Do you sing, pray, greet one another, receive sacraments, or dance in the aisles? Who would be attracted to this sort of worship? Why? Are there changes that you would like to see in worship to enrich your own experience or that you believe would attract new people?

3. *Who is currently involved?* How do age, race, and gender shape the style and practice of the congregation? Where do you come from and why did you choose your congregation? Do people tend to share a denominational background? Who is welcomed, and who seems to be excluded or not attracted to your congregation?

4. *How do you make decisions?* What decisions do the clergy make? What decisions are made by laypeople? What official and informal systems help to organize your congregation's life? Is the balance of these systems clear, and do you feel invited to be involved?

5. *What does the lens of digital culture and networked thinking reveal?* In what ways is your congregation a traditional community? What boundaries does this produce that block new people? In what ways is it fluid and accessible? What expectations do you have of visitors, and what happens if they don't meet them? What short-term opportunities to connect and engage do you offer? Do you have existing online or face-to-face networks that connect the congregation to wider communities? Does your communication invite conversation?

6. Think about both your paid staff and volunteer leaders. What are their commitments and best skills? Are they well deployed to serve the congregation's mission? Do you have needs that are not being met by your current leaders? Do leaders need training or coaching? Are there people in leadership who don't reflect the shared values of the congregation, who resist change, and who use their position to bully others? Are there gifted people who are not being invited into leadership? Why not?

7. *Who is ready to change?* What changes would address issues that you have identified and/or make you a more fluid and welcoming congregation? Are you personally ready to engage change?

QUESTIONNAIRE B: ANALYZING YOUR NEIGHBORHOOD AND NETWORKS

1. *What do you know about your geographic context?* Who are your neighbors? What is their race and language, are they young or old, queer or straight? What is their social class, how long have they been around, and how do these things shape the way they connect or resist

connection with each other? What is their religious background and what are their spiritual and social needs? How do they like to interact? What causes attract them? How are they alike and different from your congregation's insiders?

2. *What are you doing to network with your neighbors?* Do people see your congregation as a resource in the community? Why, or why not? Do you offer services to neighbors in need such as tutoring, recreation, a food bank, or immigrant support? Is your building available for neighborhood events and meetings? Does your congregation participate in community organizing and arts projects or actively meet and get to know new groups in the neighborhood? Who do you connect with? What groups are you avoiding or not connecting with? Why? What are you learning about the strengths and needs of the community, and how does this inform your mission and vision? How might these connections be strengthened?

3. *How are you involved in religious networks?* Is your congregation engaged in mission or other projects through a denomination or other consortium of congregations? Are you involved in local ecumenical and interreligious efforts? Does the congregation highlight and support emerging ministries? What are they? Do you follow teachers, preachers, or religious innovators online? What are you learning from these connections? What do the connections you choose to make suggest about the identity, mission, and vision of your congregation?

4. *Are you visible and networked online?* Do you have an informative and up-to-date website so that people can find your congregation? Does it help people looking for a church understand why they might choose yours? Is it interactive? Do your internal communications inform people and make it easy for them to connect and interact? Are you using social media (Facebook, Tik Tok, YouTube, Instagram, etc.)? Which are most likely to reach the people you are trying to network with? Are you building a congregational culture in which people share information about the congregation with their own online networks?

QUESTIONNAIRE C: CLARIFYING YOUR MISSION AND VISION

1. *What is your mission?* Your congregation's mission is a matter of who you are, who you serve, and how you do it. How did the Questionnaire A discussion of your congregation's identity and faith commitments and the Questionnaire B discussion of your surrounding community clarify your congregation's existing mission? What would you add to

better describe who you are, who you serve, and how you do it? Can you express this in a short, engaging, summary sentence or two?

2. *What is your vision?* Vision is a matter of who you want to be, what motivates you, who you want to serve, and how you intend to do it. It describes where you are going. You will want to work back and forth between the questions below because your answers to one will inform the way you think about others.

3. *What are your hopes?* How do you want to make your congregation, the larger church, and the world better? Toward what "land of milk and honey" is your exodus leading?

4. *What problems do you need to address?* What elements in your decision-making structure, style, and way of relating constrain your congregation from being its best self? Do you have commitments to property or programs that no longer serve either your existing mission or your vision of the future? Which of the needs of your surrounding community that Questionnaire B helped you explore should your congregation help to address?

5. *How will you respond to digital culture?* How is the rise of digital culture creating new challenges and opportunities for your congregation? How will you respond to the desire for looser and more fluid relationships? How can you make the congregation more open and accessible? Where can you create short-term experiences of faith and opportunities to serve and connect? How can you improve your use of digital resources and social media?

6. *With whom do you want to network?* What relationships do you seek to build within the congregation, between the congregation and the surrounding community, and with ecumenical and interfaith partners? What barriers does your congregation create or bump up against in extending your network? How will you address them?

7. *What are your biblical and theological resources?* What biblical images and stories, or theological themes and ideas, help you clarify and express your values and commitments? How do they interpret times of challenge and change? How do they clarify who God is calling you to be in this time and place? How do they shape your answers to the questions above? Are there images and themes that are no longer helpful that you would like to lay aside?

8. *How will you state your vision in a sentence or two?* Can you propose a brief version of your congregation's vision that describes who you are, where you are going, why it matters, and how your vision is motivated by an understanding of God's activity in the world?

9. *How will you turn the vision statement into an action plan?* What concrete steps will you take to live into your vision in the next three to six months and in the next year or two? Are there steps that will take longer? What changes are needed in the way you organize the congregation and make decisions, in the shape and focus of your programing, in your worship and mission life to get there? How will you lower boundaries, work on welcome without expectation, and expand your network? What changes will you make in your communications system and use of social media and how are they related to reaching the goals?

Using Digital Tools

Church as Network emphasizes the importance of understanding the rise of digital culture and the new ways that people think about their own identities, networked relationships, and leaders within it. I stress that a changing media culture creates a new missional context in which people understand and express their spiritual desires in new ways. The volume gives limited attention to the use of digital and social media per se.

Yet congregations and their leaders also need to think strategically about these tools, the way they become normative, and how their adoption will shift relationships and practices. One argument for this is that it is important for congregations and religious leaders to use the tools that the people you are trying to reach use. Certainly, the trends suggest that increasing numbers of congregations and their clergy are rapidly developing an online practice and presence.

There are good books that give more attention to this. I recommend Meredith Gould's *The Social Media Gospel: Sharing the Good News in New Ways*[1] and Keith Anderson's *Digital Cathedral: Networked Ministry in a Wireless World*.[2] Originally, I planned to create a bibliography of books on using digital media in ministry practice. However, each year the technologies change, and new books, some from major publishers, some privately published, are released. Most of them include useful information about online tools, the use of social media, producing media for worship or online use, and so forth. They often include unexplored assumptions about the nature and purpose of ministry that rest on theological assumptions that make them more useful in some settings than others. The most useful thing is for readers to use this discussion to identify areas they want to work on, think through the likely consequences of change, and ask their peers for suggestions or look for recent publications on the topic.

You don't have to become an expert on these media technologies to think about their possibilities and the way they will shape your community's ministry. But neither can you ignore them. New media cultures create entrepreneurial space where new religious practices develop and new religious leaders come to prominence. Often, their understanding of the technologies and the communities that grow up around them—or their willingness to experiment in contexts they don't yet fully understand—gives bloggers and local church webmasters the opportunity to model, interpret, and influence religious belief and practice. People who want to shape the life of traditions need to seek these people out both to understand what is happening and to stay in the conversation.

The brief discussions below can help you think about what areas of ministry you want to focus on, but those decisions are always contextual. They are driven by who you are in ministry with and what your presenting issues are.

SEGMENTATION

One characteristic of digital culture that impacts congregations is segmentation. Though the web gives you potential access to an incredible range of people, groups, and products, the algorithms that guide our paths push us toward those who are congruent with our values, tastes, and interests. The old general interest media, like *Life* magazine or *The Ed Sullivan Show*, that promised something for everyone, have been replaced by media aimed at particular interest groups. Similarly, congregations that once sought to serve everyone, sometimes at the cost of offering homogenized worship and programming, today develop styles and theologies that reach out to particular communities. So, key questions about which media to adopt and how to use it is missional include the following: Who are you called to serve? What are their media norms? How will adopting new media enable your ministry?

For people involved in forging and expressing their own religious identity, a relationship with a congregation is itself an expression of personal identity. Therefore, the congregation must have a clear and distinctive identity. Congregations often struggle against this push to differentiate themselves, suggesting that they want to be open to everyone. This expresses a theological understanding of the church as having a place for everyone. However, the desire also grows out of nostalgia for an earlier time when people largely worshipped with the closest congregation in their tradition. The desire to serve everyone and offend no one often produces bland theology and bland worship that neither excites nor goes very deep. Today congregations must have a clear theology, worldview, and style that differentiates them from others and which appeals to particular communities. Decisions they make about how to use digital media, along with the content they present, becomes part of the way the differentiate themselves.

WEBSITES

Increasingly, whether to visit at Christmas or in search of a longer-term relationship, people look for a congregation online. There are many computer programs that make establishing a website easy, and most congregations have some sort of website that at least tells potential newcomers where and when they meet. Done well, the website—in conjunction with social media use—does more. It is part of the "branding" that helps differentiate your congregation from the many others that the seeker might consider and engage. It is helpful for the website to provide a sense of the style of worship, the theological orientation of the community, its involvement in the community, and of the ways to connect with it. It does take time to establish and maintain a website so that it is useful, accurate, and up to date. You need to consider who will maintain the site. This is not just a question of who has the technical skills, for the webmaster will shape the picture of the congregation's presentation of itself. You need someone who gets your congregation's vision.

DATA MINING

Today census data and other community research is available with a click of the mouse.[3] Exploring this information can make it easier to understand who the congregation is serving. Reflection on census data can guide church planters in choosing where to locate a new ministry and how to reach out to the community where it is located. It helps existing congregations think more deeply about how their surrounding community is changing, explore who is moving in and out, and understand how the demographics of income, race, age, and religious affiliation are changing. This knowledge can help your congregation shape its program and style to speak to the people in your wider community and ponder your responsibility to those who are displaced by these changes.

COMMUNICATION

To this point, our attention has been particularly on the use of digital media to draw people into the network. But digital communication is increasingly important within the congregation as well. Costs and preference drive church newsletters online. Email lists inform people of prayer concerns or invite people to events, sermon texts are emailed to those interested, and entire services are posted online. Because digital texts are easily sampled and revised, they make it easier to offer more specialized messages to groups within your network.

These uses of digital media, useful as they may be, simply use new media to do what old media did. They are one-way communication from the institution to the individual. The real breakthrough of digital communication is that communication is no longer one way. Digital communication makes it possible to talk back to messages and for anyone in the network to be heard. Churches have been slow to adopt this possibility. Partly this is probably due to assumptions about who can and should speak for the congregation, and partly to the recognition that a wider conversation takes some monitoring—not everything someone might say belongs on your website.

SOCIAL MEDIA

In the same way that websites are becoming ubiquitous, churches increasingly have some social media presence on sites like Twitter and Facebook. But it is not enough to be there. Churches need to strategize about how and why they are using social media. For Jasper Peters, the pastor at *Belong*, a newer congregation in an old church building in Denver, "[t]he most important thing we do with social media is tell people what we value."[4] This points to a key strategy in using social media. *Belong* is using social media to reflect a particular attitude about ministry in the city, thus *Belong* and Rev. Peters articulate an urban, socially committed identity that helps people decide whether this might be a congregation they would like to connect with. To do this, Peters winnows down what he posts about. Not everything that he is interested in belongs in their feed. By focusing on those things that express *Belong*'s core values, Peters's use of social media is an expression of his own and the congregation's character and commitments.

It is not only the content of their social media that is an expression of a congregation's values. When congregations or leaders begin to use social media as part of their ministry, they embrace an open and public form of communication. This implicitly flattens the hierarchy by inviting conversation and allowing others to introduce their topics and concerns. Their participation in digital culture teaches people to expect that their voices will be honored, and if the communication within congregations and traditions is predominantly one way it seems increasing out of touch with how people communicate today. Imagine a link to the church newsletter that included space for real-time comments, corrections, and reflections. When the posting of a prayer request or invitation to participate in a service or social justice project moves from the static newsletter to the congregation's Facebook page, several significant things happen. First, the church office stops being the arbiter of what gets posted. Anyone can share their thoughts and concerns with the community. Secondly, the post becomes an opportunity for conversation. People can report that they are praying or pray online. They can ask questions about details or needs. What if the posting of a pastor's sermon included the same space for conversation that her blog does?

A further strategic issue regarding social media is whether the posts are those of the institution or of the leader. There are arguments for both approaches. A goal for a congregation is to build networks that will be sustained when leaders move on. Yet, people are more likely to feel a relationship to the leader than to an institution. This calls for clarity about your goals and some balance.

WORSHIP, IN THE SANCTUARY AND ONLINE

One place where the impact of digital technology is most evident is in the way it is used in worship. Sound systems, projection equipment, and online streaming increasingly shape the way we experience Christian worship. Here, as with other cultural and technological changes, it is important to think through the changes we are making. Technologies enhance, and draw us toward, some sensory experiences and detract from others. This encourages some forms of worship and reduces our focus on others.

Amplification made it possible to hear better and in turn encouraged the growth in the size of sanctuaries. Video projection moved our eyes from the printed bulletin to screens, which some people argue provides a more integrated group experience. It also made it possible to illustrate sermons and liturgy with still and moving images. At first these things were layered over existing worship spaces, creating the complaint that the video screen blocked worshippers' view of visual elements like the cross or stained-glass windows. Increasingly worship spaces are designed to incorporate these elements. So far, the move seems to be to relatively drab auditoriums with one or more projection screens as a distinct design element. However, religion and media theorist Stewart Hoover speculates about the possibility of worship spaces in which every surface is designed for projection.[5] Such a space could look like a medieval cathedral one week and a mountain grotto the next and incorporate movie clips or still images at will.

One by-product of online streaming has been the number of congregations that stream their services on the web. For most this seems to serve a different purpose than the televangelism of figures whose brick-and-mortar megachurches seem to exist as a backdrop for an online ministry. Rather, the streaming seems primarily aimed at and marketed to people with existing relationships to the congregation but who are ill or traveling. Streaming has also led to multiple campus congregations built around a single preaching personality.

Spectacle has long been part of worship, as anyone knows who has visited any of the great cathedrals of Europe. These developments, often combined with well-produced music, tend in that direction. Part of the tradeoff is that as worship becomes more spectacular, it becomes more something one watches and less something one participates in. Thus, as one moves toward the spectacular, congregational actions such as hymn singing, other forms of amateur music and drama, silence, the passing of the peace, and communion are deemphasized in favor of watching. There is no single right balance to these things. As your congregation plans, it is important to think through your goals in worship, to think about what is effective for a congregation of your size, and to consider what appeals to the people you want to draw and maintain.

BANKING AND GIVING

Another place where broader trends in digital culture are shaping worship practice is around the decline of a cash economy and rise of online banking. In the wider culture it has become normative, at least outside of poorer communities, to pay for almost everything with credit or debit cards. We swipe, or tap, and often no longer need to sign a receipt. Thus, the card that once was reserved for larger purchases is now used for a cup of coffee.

What are the implications for the way we contribute to congregations and recognize those gifts in worship? Many congregations now make it possible to give online. Some even have terminals outside the sanctuary where people can swipe a card. For some, between the folks who think cash is quaint and those who write a check once a month, the passing of offering baskets around the congregation is becoming a ritual increasingly cut off from the utility of collecting money for the church.

For many people, the offering seems a crucial liturgical moment. It is an opportunity to talk about a wider sense of stewardship that includes our time and our talents as well as our money. There is something satisfying about the physical act of putting our offering in the plate or bringing it forward. Having the offering placed on the altar and prayed over ritualizes in a bodily way people's commitment to give back, to support the work of the congregation, and to contribute to wider ministries.

Some congregations work to preserve this ritualized giving, even when most of their funding is gathered in other ways. Pastors invite people who have given in another way or at another time to pass the plate as a sign of those gifts. In one church with terminals in the narthex people are invited to take a card and place it the offering basket indicating that they have given online or are praying for the ministries of the church.

The moment may be coming when congregations will need to find other ways to meaningfully have these conversations. In my early teens I visited a synagogue for the first time and remember being struck by the absence of an offering. Later the rabbi explained that worship was a time set apart from everyday matters like money and that the congregation wouldn't want to embarrass those who couldn't give. Members paid dues to support the congregation. At the time it seemed strange to me, but remembering it today reminds me that gathering the money and talking about our commitments might be done in different ways that might be more congruent to our actual financial practices.

CONCLUSION

There are a wide variety of media and methods, and it matters which we choose. The axiom that "if you have a hammer everything looks like a nail" is also true of digital tools. To make wise choices that enable the healthy growth of the community and that support its mission and service, it is necessary to understand the media culture of which we are a part. As we get clear about that culture and the kind of religious desires and expressions it evokes, and as we better understand the tools available—their possibilities and limits—we are more likely to build effective ministry that networks us with others who share our journey and need our care.

Notes

ACKNOWLEDGMENTS

1. Vol. 9, 2020.
2. Jeffrey H. Mahan, *Media, Religion and Culture: An Introduction* (Abingdon: Routledge, 2014).

CHAPTER 1

1. After Hours, Denver at https://afterhoursdenver.org.
2. While I was working on this book, Herships was replaced at *After Hours, Denver* by Rev. Tyler Kaufman.
3. This is Herships's preferred term for the homeless they meet and engage within the park and on the streets.
4. Personal interview.
5. Jaroslav Pelikan, interview, *U.S. News & World Report*, July 26, 1989.
6. For an excellent discussion of the conflation of mission and colonialism, see George E. Tinker, *Missionary Conquest: The Gospel and Native American Cultural Genocide* (Minneapolis: Fortress, 1993).
7. Ross Kane, "From Africa, a Christian Case for Reverencing the Dead: Communion of Ancestors," *The Christian Century*, April 11, 2018, 30–33.
8. See Marshall McLuhan, *Understanding Media* (New York: Signet Books, 1966).
9. Printing developed earlier in Asia starting in China about 1040 and further developed in Korea in the 1370s. However, the separation of Eastern and Western cultures meant that printing developed independently in the West, and our focus here is on its impact on the shape of Western Christianity.

10. Scott Thumma, 2011, "Virtually Religious Technology and Internet Use in American Congregations," Hartford Institute for Religious Research, http://www .hartfordinstitute.org/research/technology-Internet-use.html.

11. Eric C. Smith discusses the intermingling of Jewish and Christian images in *Jewish Glass and Christian Stone: A Materialist Mapping of the Parting of the Ways* (Abingdon: Routledge, 2018).

12. William Gibson, *Neuromancer* (New York: Ace Books, 1984).

13. See Christopher Helland, "Online Religion/Religion Online and Virtual Communitas," in Jeffery K. Hadden and Douglas E. Cowan (eds.), *Religion on the Internet: Research Prospects and Promises* (New York: JAI Press, 2000), 205–24.

CHAPTER 2

1. "The Matter of Belief," in David Morgan (ed.), *Religion and Material Culture* (Abingdon: Routledge, 2010), 7–8.

2. Werner Herzog, *Cave of Forgotten Dreams*, Creative Differences Films, 2010.

3. Eric Rauth (trans.), *Media Manifestos* 44 (New York: Verso, 1996).

4. "Telegraphing Spirit," in Jeffrey H. Mahan, *Media, Religion and Culture: An Introduction* (Abingdon: Routledge, 2014), 19–20.

5. "Religious Tracts in the Eighteenth Century," in Jeffrey H. Mahan, *Media, Religion and Culture: An Introduction* (Abingdon: Routledge, 2014), 84–85.

6. For a fuller discussion, see Quentin Schultz, "Evangelical Radio and the Rise of the Electronic Church," *Journal of Broadcasting and Electronic Media*, Vol. 32 (1988), 289–306, published online May 18, 2009.

CHAPTER 3

1. David Hogue, personal conversation.

2. Stewart Hoover, personal conversation. Hoover is the director of the Center for Media, Religion and Culture, University of Colorado at Boulder.

3. See Duane Bidwell, *When One Religion Isn't Enough: The Lives of Spiritually Fluid People* (Boston: Beacon Press, 2018).

4. Article 12, *Confession of Faith in a Mennonite Perspective*, http://mennoniteusa .org/, emphasis added.

5. Katherine Turpin, personal conversation.

6. Stewart Hoover, *Religion in the Media Age* (New York: Routledge, 2006).

7. See Thomas G. Bandy, *Why Should I Believe You* (2006) and *Sideline Church* (2018, with Tex Sample), both Nashville: Abingdon Press.

8. See Jill Lepore, *These Truths: A History of the United States* (New York: W. W. Norton & Company, 2018).

9. Amy Frykholm, "Double Belonging: One Person, Two Faiths," *The Christian Century*, January 14, 2011.

10. John S. McClure, *Mashup Religion: Pop Music and Theological Invention* (Waco, TX: Baylor University Press, 2011).

11. David Morgan (ed.), "The Matter of Belief," in *Religion and Material Culture (Abingdon: Routledge, 2011),* 7–8.

12. See George E. Tinker, *Missionary Conquest: The Gospel and Native American Genocide* (Minneapolis: Augsburg Fortress, 1993).

13. Vincent J. Miller, *Consuming Religion: Christian Faith and Practice in Consumer Culture* (New York: Continuum, 2009), 29.

CHAPTER 4

1. Barbara Brown Taylor, *Learning to Walk in the Dark* (New York: HarperOne, 2014), 145.

2. Pete Ward, *Liquid Church* (Peabody: Hendrickson Publishers, 2002), 16.

3. Robert Putnam and David Campbell, *American Grace: How Religion Divides and Unites Us* (New York: Simon & Schuster, 2010), 126.

4. Jeffrey M. Jones, "US Church Membership Down Sharply in Past Two Decades," Gallup, https://news.gallup.com/poll/248837/church-membership-down-sharply-past-two-decades.aspx.

5. "Community," https://www.merriam-webster.com/dictionary/community.

6. The concept of *habitus* was laid out by French sociologist Pierre Bourdieu. For a summary, see https://www.encyclopedia.com/social-sciences-and-law/sociology-and-social-reform/sociology-general-terms-and-concepts/habitus.

7. Heidi Campbell, "Understanding the Relationships between Religion Online and Offline in a Networked Society," *Journal of the American Academy of Religion* 80, no. 1 (March 2012): 65.

8. Heidi Campbell, "Challenges Created by Online Religious Networks," *Journal of Media and Religion* 3, no. 2 (2004): 84.

9. Manuel Castells, cited in Pete Ward, *Liquid Church* (Peabody: Hendrickson Publishers, 2002), 4.

10. Personal conversations, Fall of 2019, with Michael Hemenway and Ted Vial, at Iliff School of Theology's Artificial Intelligence Institute.

11. Deanna Thompson, *The Virtual Body of Christ in a Suffering World* (Nashville: Abingdon Press, 2016); see especially chapter 1.

12. On February 14, 2018, a former student opened fire with a semiautomatic rifle at Marjory Stoneman Douglas High School in Parkland, Florida, killing seventeen people and injuring seventeen others.

13. Mepkin Abbey, advertisement in *The Christian Century*, October 10, 2018, 40.

14. David Teutsch, *Spiritual Community: The Power to Restore Hope, Commitment, and Joy* (Woodstock: Jewish Lights Publishing, 2005); see especially chapter 4.

CHAPTER 5

1. Marcel Proust, *À la recherche du temps perdu*, published in seven volumes between 1913 and 1927, first translated as *Remembrance of Things Past*.

2. The movement, most influential in the late twentieth century and early twenty-first, seeks to create a postmodern conversation that brings together liberal and conservative Protestants experimenting with new forms of congregation and community. They are critiqued for being a predominantly white conversation. Leading figures include Tony Jones, Brian McLaren, and Doug Pagitt.

3. "Networked Church," *Movement Magazine*, Issues 116 and 117, 2004, http://www.smallritual.org/section4/networkchurch1.html.

4. The research was organized by the Center for Media, Religion, and Culture located at the College of Media, Communication, and Information at the University of Colorado at Boulder, https://www.colorado.edu/cmrc/.

5. Momastery.com.

6. David Hogue, personal conversation.

7. "Authority," https://www.etymonline.com/word/authority.

8. Rowan Williams, *Arius: Heresy and Tradition* (Grand Rapids, MI: Eerdmans, 1987).

CHAPTER 6

1. Jeremy Garber, *Another Way: Thinking Together about the Holy Spirit* (Eugene, OR: Pickwick Publications, 2019), 1, 31, and 143.

2. Serena Jones, *Feminist Theory and Christian Theology: Cartographies of Grace* (Minneapolis: Fortress Press, 2000), 172.

3. Rowan Williams, *Arius: Heresy and Tradition* (Grand Rapids, MI: Eerdmans, 1987).

4. PBS, *The Black Church: This Is Our Story, This Is Our Song*, https://www.pbs.org/weta/black-church/watch.

5. Jason Byassee, "Two Vibrant Anglican Congregations in Winnipeg," *The Christian Century* (December 19, 2018), 33.

6. Deanna A. Thompson, *The Virtual Body of Christ in a Suffering World* (Nashville: Abingdon, 2016).

7. Thompson, *The Virtual Body of Christ*, 3, 4.

8. Thompson, 41, citing Byassee, "For Virtual Theological Education," *Faith and Leadership* (March 2, 2011), http://www.faithandleadership.com/blog/03-02-2011/jason-byassee-for-virtual-theological-education.

9. David Hogue, personal correspondence, March 23, 2021.

CHAPTER 7

1. Tom Bandy, personal conversation.

2. Steven Collins, "Networked Church," *Movement Magazine* 116 and 117 (2004), http://www.smallritual.org/section4/networkchurch1.html.

3. Harvard Divinity School, *How We Gather*, https://www.howwegather.org. See the report "Something More."

4. Pete Ward, *Liquid Church* (Eugene, OR: Wipf and Stock Publishers, 2002), 2.

CHAPTER 8

1. Nadia Bolz-Weber, class visit.

2. Peter Ward, *Liquid Church* (Peabody: Hendrickson Publishers, 2002).

3. For an early exploration of this shift and its importance, see Christopher Helland, "Online Religion/Religion Online and Virtual Communitas," in Jeffery K. Hadden and Douglas E. Cowan (eds.), *Religion on the Internet: Research Prospects and Promises* (New York: JAI Press, 2000).

4. Katherine Turpin, personal conversation about her forthcoming work.

5. Judaism Your Way, https://www.facebook.com/JudaismYourWayPage.

6. For an example, see the Chicago Temple, a United Methodist Congregation that occupies the top and bottom of an urban high-rise at https://openhousechicago.org/sites/site/first-united-methodist-church-at-the-chicago-temple/.

APPENDIX 2

1. Meredith Gould, *The Social Media Gospel: Sharing the Good News in New Ways* (Collegeville, MN: Liturgical Press, 2015).

2. Keith Anderson, *Digital Cathedral: Networked Ministry in a Wireless World* (New York: Morehouse Publishing, 2015).

3. Census data is available at no charge directly from the U.S. government. See https://www.census.gov/data/data-tools.html. There are also services that, for a price, will interpret and package the data for congregations and not-for-profits. For a good example of such a program, see MissionInsite https://www.missioninsite.com/.

4. Jasper Peters, quoted in "Finding Faith in Our Colorado," KMGH-TV, aired December 23, 2018.

5. Stewart Hoover, personal conversation.

Index

About the Author

Jeffrey H. Mahan is the Ralph E. and Norma E. Peck Professor of Religion and Communication at the Iliff School of Theology in Denver, Colorado, and a resident fellow at the Center for Media, Religion and Culture at the University of Colorado Boulder.

Mahan studies the mediation of religion in material and digital cultures, religion as a sensual and bodily experience, and the implications of media change for the practice of ministry and religious leadership. He is interested in aesthetic and theological engagements with both fine and popular film, literature, and television. This has led to appointments to ecumenical juries at the Montreal, Cannes, and Berlin film festivals. He is also interested in the history of media and mediation and their implications for religious communities and practices, with particular attention to the emergence of digital culture and the forms of religion in digital culture. An ordained United Methodist minister, he earlier served as pastor of urban congregations in Chicago.

Mahan was founding cochair of the Religion and Popular Culture Group of the American Academy of Religion. He is also a member of the International Society for Media, Religion, and Culture. He serves on the editorial board, for the *Journal of Religion and Popular Culture*. He is often a source for journalists covering popular culture and religion in the current media age.

His publications include *Religion and Popular Culture in America, Revised and Expanded Third Edition* (2017), *Media, Religion and Culture: An Introduction* (2014), *Shared Wisdom* (1993), *A Long Way from Solving That One* (1990), and *American Television Genres* (1985) as well as articles and book chapters.